Interactive Computing in BASIC

Interactive Computing in BASIC
An introduction to interactive computing and a practical course in the BASIC language

PETER C. SANDERSON, M.A.

Advisory Officer (Computers)
LAMSAC
(Local Authorities Management
Services and Computer Committee)

First Edition

petrocelli
books

New York, 1973

© Butterworth & Co (Publishers) Ltd, 1973

First US edition published by Petrocelli Books, division of Mason & Lipscomb Publishers, Inc., New York City, 1973

International Standard Book Number: 0−88405−019−X
Library of Congress Catalog Card Number: 73−11244

Library of Congress Cataloging in Publication Data

Sanderson, Peter C
Interactive computing in BASIC.

1. Basic (Computer program language) I. Title.
QA76.73.B3S26   001.6'424   73−11244
ISBN 0−88405−019−X

Made and printed in Great Britain

CONTENTS

1	Introduction to Computers	1
2	Aspects of Terminal Usage	16
3	Programming Languages	25
4	Stages in Writing and Testing a Program	32
5	Introduction to the BASIC Language	43
6	How to Write Simple Arithmetical Programs in BASIC	55
7	Control Statements in the BASIC Language	70
8	Loops and Subscripted Variables	84
9	Functions and Subroutines	95
10	Further Printing Facilities and Character Manipulation	106
11	Matrix Instructions	115
12	Versions of BASIC	121
13	From BASIC to FORTRAN	123
	Suggested Solutions	138
	Index	159

Chapter 1

INTRODUCTION TO COMPUTERS

The computer is coming to dominate contemporary life in the same way as the steam engine ruled the lives of our early-Victorian ancestors. The present age has already been defined as a Cybernetic Revolution which has considerable analogies with the nineteenth century Industrial Revolution.

In most aspects of our daily lives we now encounter computers. They are used extensively for the production of commercial bills, demands and statements and within industry for production control, stock control and sales accounting. Computers are also used extensively for local and central government purposes such as rate accounting, national insurance records and census analysis. There is a growing use of computers for the control of traffic lights and other uses in transport include airline seat reservation, air traffic control, motorway and bridge design and, in some countries, railway seat reservations. You can see that a computer is a highly versatile machine to accomplish the above tasks. These are only a small part of the myriad applications for which a computer has been found useful. The U.S. Space Research Programme would have been impossible to carry out without the rapid calculating power of the computer, whilst we sleep at nights under an anti-missile umbrella dependent on the computer. Computers have been used for such diverse tasks as dating and marriage bureaux, medical diagnosis, musical composition and machine tool control. In the same way as a car driver does not have to understand the intricacies of the internal-combustion engine to drive a car so the computer can be used for many disparate applications without detailed knowledge of its inner electronic working.

The computer is especially useful for technical and scientific work since it eliminates the drudgery of complex calculations. In fact many computations which would have never been attempted previously are now performed with ease with the aid of the computer. Some of the technical application areas where computer usage has proved highly successful are listed in *Table 1.1*.

You may wonder what kind of a machine the computer is in view of its ability to perform all the tasks mentioned so far in this chapter. The digital computer (analogue and hybrid computers have no relevance to

Table 1.1. *Technical applications of computers*

Aeronautical Engineering

Airframe stress analysis	Critical speed problems
Flight simulation	Flight test data reduction
Flutter analysis	Gyroscopic calculations
Heat transfer analysis	Satellite tracking
Vibration analysis	Wind-tunnel data reduction

Chemistry and Chemical Engineering

Crystal structure factors	Equilibrium equations
Flash vapour calculations	Gas line calculation
Mass spectrometer analysis	Spectrum analysis

Civil Engineering

Abutment design	Beam design
Bridge design	Concrete design
Construction tie computations	Cut and fill calculations
Cylindrical shell analysis	Dam design
Earthwork calculations	Embankment stability design
Highway profiles	Pavement design
Photogrammetric data reduction	Pier design
Pipe design	Retaining-wall design
Roadway elevations	Soil test analysis
Stress analysis	Traffic simulation
Traverse adjustment	Traverse closure

Electrical Engineering

Antenna design	Circuit analysis and design
Component design	Filter analysis
Generator calculations	Logical-network design
Motor calculations	Radar echoes
Radio interference	Transformer design

Hydraulic Engineering

Backwater profiles	Drainage system design
Flood forecasting	Open channel flow
Network analysis	Pipe stresses
Reservoir area calculations	Sewer design
Storm-sewer analysis	Surge-tank analysis
Water-hammer analysis	Wave motion analysis

Introduction to Computers

Mathematics

Calculus of variations
Curve fitting
Difference equations
Eigenvalues and eigenvectors
Integral equations
Least squares
Multiple integrals
Polynomial roots
Simultaneous non-linear equations

Convolution
Determinant evaluation
Differential equations
Fourier analysis
Lagrange interpolation
Matrix arithmetic and inversion
Partial differential equations
Simultaneous linear equations
Table computation

Mechanical Engineering

Air conditioning calculations
Hardy–Cross analysis
Casing design
Heat flow
Moments of inertia
Pressure-vessel calculations
Shell analysis

Arch analysis and design
Cam design
Crankshaft vibration analysis
Machine vibration analysis
Pipe stress analysis
Rigid body vibrations
Truss analysis

Physics

Colour analysis
Electron trajectories
Shock wave analysis

Crystallography analysis
Neutron transport
Themodynamic equations

Statistics

Beta functions
Correlation
Factor analysis
Gamma functions
Moving averages
Poisson probability
Time series analysis
Regression analysis

Binominal coefficient calculations
Covariance
Forecasting
Gaussian probability
Multiple regression analysis
Principal component analysis
Analysis of variance
Survey analysis

this book) may be defined as an electronic machine for the processing of numerical or symbolic data in a predetermined manner without operator intervention. All calculating machines except for the computer are limited to the manipulation of numeric data and need perpetual operator interventions: thus their speed is dependent on the reaction of the human operator to previously displayed results. No other calculating machine apart from the computer will be able to perform such tasks as language translation or textual analysis. The facility which gives the computer the power of proceeding through its manipulation of data without operator intervention is its power of obeying a stored program. All the instructions for a specific task are read into the computer and then (on a simple computer, although the principle is the same on the most complex and expensive computer) the instructions in the program are obeyed one after the other without any need for an operator to press buttons after the examination of intermediate results. The electronic nature of the computer means that arithmetic and symbol manipulation is performed at electronic speeds so that a million simple operations may be performed in a second.* The list of instructions to perform a desired task is known as a *program* and without this a computer is little more than a costly and inert mass of metal. Computers can be programmed skilfully without a knowledge of the electronic basis of computer design so that this book will not enter into discussion of the intricacies of gates and flip-flops or of binary arithmetic. A high-level programming language such as BASIC successfully conceals the electronic workings of the computer.

It must be emphasised that a computer is entirely dependent upon its program, which gives the logical steps for the solution of a specific problem. Any task which cannot be reduced to a series of logical steps cannot become a computer program. It is perfectly feasible for a computer to be programmed or instructed in machine code to modify and alter its instructions during the course of a program. This facility of modifying instructions during the solution of a problem is the basis of the heuristic or "learning" programs whereby computers have been programmed to play chess or draughts (checkers) and prove geometrical theorems. One of the most vital instructions in the repertoire of any computer is the conditional or branching instruction whereby the computer can follow instructions along one or other path as a result of a test of an intermediate result. Therefore in solving quadratic equations a computer can be programmed to print that the roots are not real if $4ac > b^2$.

Although any problem which can be reduced to a series of logical steps can be represented as a computer program or sequence of instructions, there are certain problems which are ideally suited to computer solution. Any problems such as the inversion of large matrices, where solution by any other method of computation would take up too much time and effort, can ideally take advantage of the electronic arithmetic speeds of the computer. Problems involving repetitive manipulation of large volumes of data are also suited to computer processing. The great

---

* Common time measurements used in computing are: *microsecond* (μs) for a millionth of a second, *millisecond* (ms) for a thousandth of a second and *nanosecond* (ns) for a thousand-millionth of a second.

Introduction to Computers

majority of commercial computer applications such as payroll and invoicing fall into this category. There is a class of computer (or data processing) applications which do little computation but rely on the vast amount of data which a computer can store and on the high speed of its retrieval. Applications which use the computer as a rapid electronic filing system are generally classed as information systems. Some of the earliest applications of this type were concerned with airline seat reservations. It is impossible to be too dogmatic as to whether or not a particular application is suitable for a computer. Individual circumstances play a large part in the determination of whether a problem is to be solved on a computer or by other means. If a research worker is racing against time it is worthwhile to use a computer to solve problems which in other circumstances may be considered too trivial. Generally, computers are ideal for applications involving large amounts of data; requiring rapid retrieval from a large mass of information, or demanding accurate computation of problems too lengthy for alternative methods of solution. Modern computers are so constructed that they will not proceed with a calculation if there is any malfunction in their inner electronics. The computer "mistakes" so avidly publicised are due to faulty input data or wrong instructions in the program.

The idea of a calculating machine with a stored program which could work through a problem without operator intervention first appeared in the early-Victorian era in the work of Charles Babbage. His idea of an Analytical Engine had a stored program on punched cards, based on the cards used in the Jacquard loom, which eliminated operator intervention during the programmed calculation. The machine was designed to work to 50 decimal places but contemporary engineering techniques were totally inadequate to construct the Analytical Engine according to his design. Babbage himself designed new forms of machine tool to assist in the construction of the machine but relatively little was accomplished.

The first electronic digital computer was ENIAC: this was developed at the University of Pennsylvania in 1946 for the solution of ballistic problems, so that electronic computers are younger in development than plastics or radar. This first computer used valves and was extremely heavy and bulky. The first general-purpose computer marketed was UNIVAC I which was put on sale by the Sperry Rand Corporation in 1951. From then until 1959 more and more different types of computers appeared on the market, known as first-generation computers: these all used valves and so were bulky and needed expensive air-conditioning.

The second generation of computers spans the years 1959—64. The important change in computer construction between first- and second-generation machines was replacement of the valves by transistors, which enabled computers to become smaller and cheaper. Printed circuits replaced bulky wires and computation became many times faster.

The current types of computer you will meet are sometimes referred to as third-generation computers. The main improvements since the second generation have been even greater compactness owing to extensive use of integrated circuits and micro-miniaturised techniques. A chip of silicon can contain an integrated circuit which is equivalent to several circuits composed of transistors, diodes, capacitors and their connections. The connection of these integrated circuits by multi-layer printed circuits saves cumbrous wiring. Speeds have increased from microseconds to nanoseconds.

All the computers you are likely to encounter are general-purpose computers which can be used with equal facility for mathematical computations, commercial data processing, textual analysis or language translation. The component features of the computer which will be relevant to your use of a computer terminal will now be discussed. The physical units of a computer are known as "hardware", in contrast to the programs which are generically known as "software".

Certain basic functional units are common to all computers from the small "mini-computers" to giants such as the IBM System 370/165. Before the functional parts of a computer are examined it is interesting to consider the analogy of how you would perform a computation requiring many steps. Obviously you would have some initial numbers on which to perform the desired calculations. This is analogous to computer *input* in the same way as the means by which you write your final result and any headings or explanation is analogous to computer *output*. (Any tables you use are equivalent to the computer *file store* or *backing store*.) The list of instructions you perform is like the computer *program* and your memory which contains the instructions, the data items on which you are actually working and the intermediate results is like the computer *store* or *memory*. Your facility of doing arithmetic has its parallel in the computer *arithmetic unit*. Your ability to perform the instructions in sequence and to translate them into arithmetical processes is analogous to the *control unit*.

Figure 1.1 shows the movement of data and of control information in a computer. Input is decoded and placed by the control unit in the store or memory from which output information comes when the appropriate instructions occur in the program. The store holds the program as well as data. Instructions are taken in sequence by the control unit which initiates the appropriate circuitry of the arithmetic unit, file device, or input/output units. Input, output and file devices are often referred to as *peripherals*. The memory, control unit and arithmetic unit are often housed together in the same cabinet and are collectively known as the central processor, central processing unit or

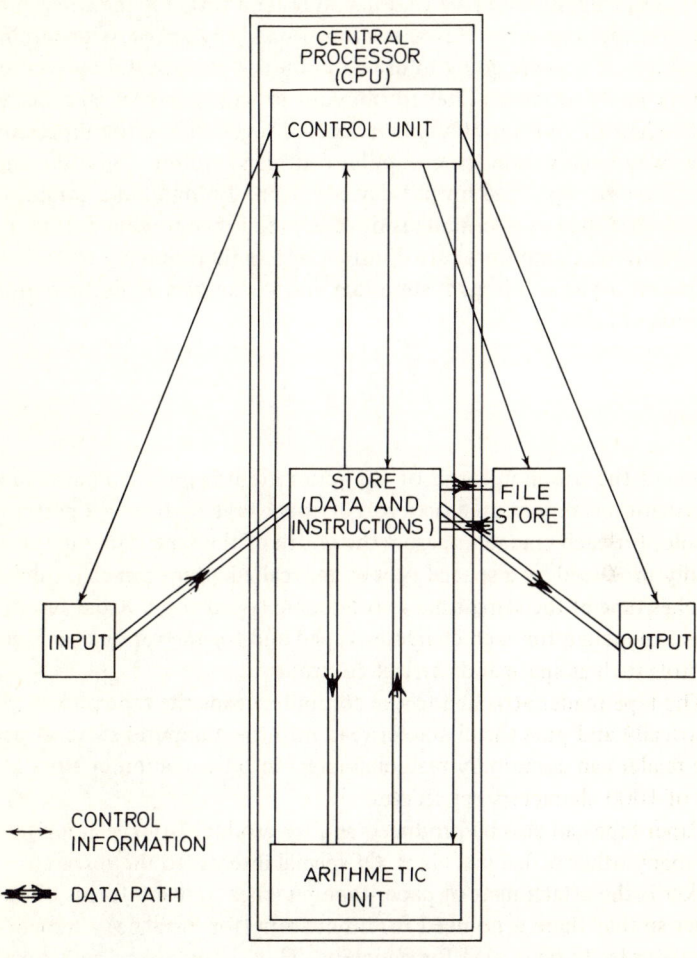

Figure 1.1 Components of a computing system

CPU. You can think of your terminal (which will be described in greater detail in the next chapter) as both an input and output unit.

Until the recent development of terminals the only method of computer usage was known as *batch-processing*. This involved a batch of input been processed in its entirety in the computer room. Terminals make it possible for input to be entered as it occurs and for a remote user to work interactively in the form of a dialogue with the central computer. You will experience this yourself when you write your first programs in BASIC and find that if you enter a formally incorrect program statement an error message will be quickly typed on your terminal typewriter. If you are going to use computers a great deal, however, you are very likely sooner or later to run your programs in a batch-processing mode when all your input will be collected together and the processing done away from you in the computer centre. Therefore, the following description of input and output devices primarily found in a computer room rather than at a terminal is of direct relevance to your future use of computers. Computers vary considerably in their number of peripheral devices. A large system may have examples of all the peripherals mentioned below.

Input

1. One of the common forms of computer input is punched paper tape. Information is represented on a roll of paper tape by having a pattern of holes for each character across the width of the tape. The tape is usually produced by a special typewriter (called a tape-punch) which punches tape at the same time as producing typed copy. A pattern of holes is punched for each character typed and for the various carriage controls such as space and carriage return.

The tape reader attached to the computer reads the tape photoelectrically and puts the character read into the computer store. A paper-tape reader can commonly read characters into the computer store at a rate of 1000 characters per second.

Paper tape can also be produced as a by-product from cash registers and many other office machines. Of special interest to the research worker is the attachment of paper-tape punches to many forms of data logger so that there is no need for input from (for instance) a temperature recorder to be copied for punching. Thus, copying and punching time is saved and transcription errors are eliminated.

Introduction to Computers

When tapes are punched from written or printed copy they are invariably verified so that (theoretically) no wrong data is presented to the computer. Verification is done by the re-punching of the original information, character by character, on a typewriter which compares each character with the corresponding character in the first tape that was punched. The keyboard locks if the characters on the two tapes do not correspond.

Most terminals can produce paper tape if desired. The use of paper tape in a terminal environment will be discussed in the next chapter.

2. The other common form of computer input is the punched card. The card in most common use has 80 columns. Characters are represented by a punch or combination of punches in a single column which contains 12 punching positions. The way in which certain columns are used in the preparation of programs in the computer language FORTRAN is described on page 124.

Cards are prepared on a card punch, which is larger than a paper-tape punch. A card verifier compares holes on the card originally punched with the keys pressed by the operator: if they do not correspond an indication is given. Punched cards can also be produced as a by-product from office machines and data loggers. Cards are read into the computer store by a card reader, a card reader working at speeds from 300 to 2000 cards a minute.

3. Sometimes input is transcribed to magnetic tape by a special key-device known as a tape encoder. It is possible to read magnetic tape into the computer at a much faster rate than punched cards or paper tape but the use of this medium of input is chiefly confined to commercial data processing applications with large volumes of input data.

4. Various types of magnetic character readers (which read the hieroglyphics at the bottoms of cheques) and optical character readers are used for commercial work. Readers which read marks in pre-determined sections on a form are sometimes used in recording surveys for the statistician.

Output

1. The chief form of output that you will encounter at your terminal is the typewriter. A computer centre has various output devices such as

card punches and tape punches which are unlikely to be relevant to your use of computers. Equally irrelevant, but more exotic, is the audio-response unit which transmits a verbal reply (in a feminine Harvard accent) along telephone lines. A graph-plotter can be attached to a computer and can naturally produce more accurate graphs than the histograms which it is possible to produce at your terminal typewriter.

2. If you are using a terminal for your BASIC programs your output is not likely to be printed on a line-printer. This prints a line at a time in contrast to a teleprinter which prints only a character at a time. Speeds for a line-printer range from 300 to 2000 lines a minute. Typical line-printer output can be seen in public-utility bills.

There are two types of line-printer: the chain printer and the barrel printer. In a chain printer, the characters are embossed on the outer edge of a metal chain that revolves continuously past the paper. The print characters of a barrel printer appear in each print position on the circumference of a solid metal barrel. When the desired character passes the appropriate print position, a hammer presses the paper against a carbon ribbon which separates the paper and the characters. Although the chain or barrel is continuously rotating, you will see, if you examine computer-produced bills or other documents, that the printing is clear thanks to the high speed of the hammers. Printing is done on continuous stationery (often pre-printed with headings in commercial applications) which is guided through the printer by sprocket holes at the edges of the paper. The continuous roll of paper is divided into sheets by semi-perforated divisions. The most common length of line of the printer is 132 characters. Various character sets according to requirements can be obtained.

3. Visual display units are in fairly common use as terminals so that this method of computer output will be discussed in the next chapter.

The Main Store

This is alternatively referred to as the memory and is used to store program instructions, data and intermediate results. The most usual form of storage uses magnetic cores so that the main store is often called the core store although some computers now use speedier and more compact forms of storage. The most common unit of store is the *byte* which

Introduction to Computers

contains 8 binary digits or bits and can be used to hold two decimal digits or a single alphanumeric character. Other units of store are known to users of specific computers as *words* (which in one computer hold a number or 4 characters) and *characters* (which on one computer contain 6 bits). The size of a computer store is commonly referred to as so many "K" where K represents 1024 units of storage. Usually, computer memories are built with a number of units which is an exact power of two, so that a 16K memory contains 16 384 units and a 64K memory contains 65 536 units. The exact binary form in which information is held varies considerably in specific types of computer. There is naturally a limit as to the largest and smallest numbers which can be represented and which can be transferred to the arithmetic unit.

The bytes or other units of store can be regarded as pigeon-holes for the storage of data or instructions. Each unit can be considered as having a unique address which is used by program instructions when it is desired to work on information in that particular unit of store so that (on some computers) an addition instruction referring to units 1700 and 1850 would add the contents of those units of computer store together.

Information transferred to or from a store address is automatically checked for any malfunction which would result in a bit being lost or gained.

The speed at which information can be accessed in the computer store is one of the principal factors which determine the speed of the computer. Most computer specifications give the *cycle time* of the store. This is the time taken to read the contents of any address in the main store. Average cycle times are in the region of a microsecond although for some computers the cycle time is now measured in nanoseconds.

Main store is expensive and so cannot practicably be used for the files used in commercial data processing or to store your terminal programs when you are not using them. Therefore some form of backing store, auxiliary memory or file store is needed to supplement the capacity of the main store.

Backing Store

The terminal user has no control over the form of backing store used. The following information will be of use to programmers using a batch-processing system.

1. Magnetic tape is probably the most common form of backing store. Usually ½ in wide it is like the tape used in audio tape recorders and is commonly processed in 800 m reels. Information is written from store to tape and is read back into the store when needed. You are not likely to encounter tape a great deal in your technical computing at a typewriter terminal. To find data towards the end of the tape, all previous information has to be passed over. The time taken to do this prevents tape providing a suitable backing store for interactive working.

2. Exchangeable magnetic discs are most useful in terminal working since the average access time to retrieve a record is much shorter. File storage units such as exchangeable disc units or (to use the conventional terminology) *disc-drives* are generically known as random access devices or direct access devices. The time taken to access a record on such devices is, unlike the case with magnetic tape units, relatively independent of the position of the information accessed on the file. The most common form of random access uses packs of metallic discs which are coated on each side with a magnetic recording material. These packs (commonly of 6 or 11 discs) can be removed and replaced on a disc-drive in less than 1 min. A pack of 6 discs contains typically 7¼ million bytes. The average time to find a record here is 87.5 ms. (The average time to find a record on a magnetic tape unit is half the length of time it takes to pass through a whole reel of tape; often a time in the region of 2½ min!) A common disc-drive has a read—write head for each disc surface and these are mounted on an arm between each pair of surfaces. The discs continuously rotate and the read—write heads move up and down the arms to position themselves over the selected record.

Exchangeable disc packs at the central computer installation are ideal for users at remote terminals. It takes little time for the operator to put the disc containing your programs and data on a drive if it is not already on a drive. Some disc packs are of considerably greater capacity than 7¼ million bytes. One recent pack has a data capacity of 100 million bytes and an average access time of 30 ms.

3. There are also fixed disc units where the discs cannot be exchanged or replaced. These are usually of greater capacity than the exchangeable discs and useful for holdings sections of important systems programs to enable the computer system to work in a highly efficient manner. The process of translating your BASIC program into the machine language of

Introduction to Computers

the computer involves the use of a program known as a *compiler* (which will be discussed in Chapter 3). The use of a fixed disc to hold sections of the compiler makes for very fast translation. These fixed discs often have one read–write head per track. One such system has average access times between 17 ms and 60 ms and can have a maximum size of 38 billion bytes.

4. Some installations use magnetic drums instead of fixed discs. Data is recorded in parallel tracks on the magnetic surface of a drum and there is often a single head per track.

Arithmetic Unit

This unit contains the circuitry to perform arithmetic operations. The sophistication of the arithmetic unit varies from one computer to another. Some arithmetic units will not perform multiplication and division which are performed by instructions in the program. Calculations are performed by the arithmetic unit under the direction of the control unit. Some computers have a special register known as an *accumulator* which is used in arithmetic operations for accumulation of arithmetic results.

Computers which are going to be used for work with calculations involving decimal fractions or for very large or very small numbers have special circuitry, which can be optionally fitted to the great majority of computers on the market, to assist the programmer in representing these numbers and in keeping track of the decimal point after successive multiplications and divisions. The facility offered by this special circuitry is known as *floating point* representation of numbers and floating point arithmetic. The developments of modern science have led to the use of very large numbers, such as inter-planetary distances and populations of pathogenic bacteria, and very small numbers such as the weight of an electron and the wave-length of light. A typical number which may be encountered is the number of atoms in 1.008 g of hydrogen which is:

$$606\ 000\ 000\ 000\ 000\ 000\ 000\ 000$$

Such numbers cannot be expressed in normal binary notation owing to the number of bits (or binary digits) they would occupy, so that floating point representation is essential.

Floating point numbers are represented in a logarithmic form involving an argument and an exponent. If n represents the desired number, a the argument, b the exponent and c the base then

$$n = a \cdot c^b$$

The base is often 2, 8, 16 or 10 and it is customary to have the argument as a fraction, so that with a base of 2 typical floating point representations would be:

Number (n)	Exponent (b)	Argument (a)
$c = 2$		
1	1	.5
240	8	.9375
−.078125	−3	−.625

so that

$$1 = .5 \times 2^1 = .5 \times 2$$
$$240 = .9375 \times 2^8 = .9375 \times 256$$
$$-.078125 = -.625 \times 2^{-3} = -.625 \times .125$$

Since the storage of the exponent and argument occupy fewer bits than would be used to store the number in binary notation you can see that the use of floating point representation extends the range of numbers which can be used.

The Control Unit

The control unit directs all the activities of the computer. It ensures that operations are performed in the desired sequence. Signals are initiated to the circuitry to perform the appropriate operations, which are coordinated and timed so that a smooth flow of information is assured.

The chief work of the control unit is defined below.

1. To start and stop the computer.
2. To detect error conditions (such as an attempt to perform an impossible arithmetic operation such as the extraction of the square root of a negative number).

3. To generate the pulses which control the timing of operations.
4. To transmit pulses to the store to obtain the appropriate instructions and the operands on which the instructions are to work.
5. To decode the instructions and pass the relevant signals to the arithmetic unit or peripheral circuitry.

All the essential components of the computer have now been discussed. The next chapter will discuss the terminal environment when you will be able to see the relevance of some of these functional units to your use of the terminal. It will also describe the essential function of programs or systems software supplied by the manufacturer in ensuring that the various components of a computer system work together as an efficient whole.

Chapter 2

ASPECTS OF TERMINAL USAGE

Terminals like the one you use are connected to the central computer, the functional parts of which were described in the previous chapter. You may wonder why the work you do is never confused with the work done by other terminal users and with the batch-processing work of the central computer installation which is being undertaken whilst you are using your terminal. If you are using BASIC in a batch-processing mode on a large computer it is likely that the execution of your program is shared with other programs so that, when you are using a printer at 600 lines a minute, you are not leaving the central processor, which may have a cycle time of a microsecond, idle till your printing is completed. The technique which allows several batch or terminal programs to be run at the same time in the central processor is known as multi-programming.

Multi-programming

It is vital that a terminal system uses a central processor which has a large enough store to accommodate several programs and also the program which is supplied by the manufacturers to ensure that the various programs never interfere with one another and it is also vital that the central processor and peripherals are used so that there is a minimum of idle time. The manufacturer's program is part of the *systems software* supplied to ensure that the computer is used to its best advantage. This program is usually referred to as an *Operating System* since it minimises operator intervention; it is also sometimes referred to as the Executive Program or the System Supervisor.

Typical operating systems suitable for configurations involving terminal usage are MCP for Burroughs computers, Mod 4 for Honeywell, OS for IBM, George III for ICL and Exec 8 for Univac.

Aspects of Terminal Usage 17

This operating system occupies space in the main store, and in some cases on disc storage as well, so that this space must be taken into account in the choice of a computer suitable for running more than a single program at a time.

These operating systems share processor times between programs in the computer in various different ways. Some will commence computing on another program the moment the original program initiates a peripheral transfer of information which is slow compared with arithmetic speeds. Some operating systems designed for a terminal environment will allot a small fraction of time to each active terminal and will attend to each active terminal in rotation. The interval of time you take between the typing of one character and the next is adequate for attention to be paid to several terminals or for a considerable amount of computation to be performed on other programs in the central processor.

Operating systems were originally designed so that more than a single batch-processing program could run at the same time and they are not a product of the growth in terminal usage even though they are essential to terminal working. All operating systems have some arrangements whereby a certain program or a certain terminal can be given priority in processing so that other work is suspended whenever that program needs to use the central processor. Some common functions of operating systems are:

loading and controlling the running of programs,
displaying error and exception messages to the operator,
scheduling priorities and the execution of programs,
controlling peripherals as required by programs,
suspending a program if it cannot proceed,
ensuring optimum use of the configuration,
arranging for transfer of sections of program between a random access device and the main store,
ensuring that a program works with correct files.

If you attempt to read more data than you have input or try to divide by zero you will have a message initiated by the operating system typed at your terminal.

Whether you are using a remote terminal or running your programs at the central computer installation in a multi-programming system, the operating system enables you to feel that your program is the only one in the computer system. If by accident you attempt to interfere with another program the running of your program will be immediately suspended and an appropriate error message displayed. The operating system takes complete charge of the complex housekeeping of running your program in a multi-programming environment and you will never know how many times your program has been transferred from main store to disc so that other programs could make use of the main store.

To all intents and purposes you have the power of a large computer at your finger-tips. For many types of calculation your terminal behaves as though you had a computer on the premises. The computer to which you have access is likely to be far more powerful than the computer which would be feasible for you to use solely.

Operating Systems in a Terminal Environment

The kind of computing in which you are involved if you are using a terminal is known as *multi-access* or *time-sharing* computing and a computer configuration which supports terminals is known as a multi-access system. Computing so that you can obtain an immediate response is known as *interactive* computing. The term *real-time* computing, which was originally applied to immediate response to signals in computer-controlled process control systems and radar systems, is also used to describe this facility of immediate response.

It has already been mentioned that operating systems were originally designed to allow several batch-processing programs to run concurrently. An operating system to deal with a multi-access system must have additional facilities to those functions described above. These extra features are sometimes known as communications software. Some necessary facilities of a multi-access operating system are:

assembling messages from the various terminals,
allocating time to the various terminals,
ensuring that only legitimate users make use of terminal facilities and that only authorised users access certain files,
ensuring that failure does not produce irrecoverable damage to data and programs and the orderly continuation of the processing of messages interrupted by a fault,
ensuring that terminals receive attention when activated.

Aspects of Terminal Usage

The initial statements which you type in at the terminal typewriter whereby you identify yourself and satisfy the system that you are a legitimate user are serviced by the communications software.

Terminals

The terminal which you are most likely to use is in the form of a typewriter keyboard which types only in capitals since the shift key will enable the special characters at the top of the keys (such as / over L) to be used. It is worth noting at this point that all numerals (unlike the conventional typewriter keyboard) are on the top line so that if you type capital O for zero an error will result. The annoying and infuriating position of = in the shift must be noticed so that the use of the shift key is essential for such simple BASIC statements as

    100   LET A = 7

which beginners often type as:

    100   LET A − 7

A diagram of a typical keyboard is shown in *Figure 2.1*. Special keyboards, oriented towards specific applications, are sometimes found.

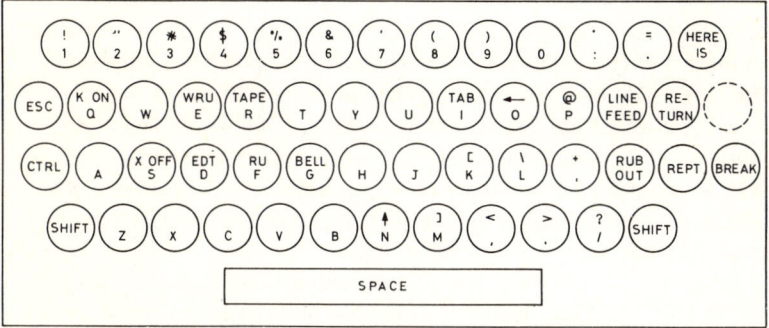

Figure 2.1 Diagram of a typical computer typewriter keyboard

This terminal is used to print messages and results from the computer as well as for your transmitted data and programs. Typing speeds of the output are slow (a common speed is 10 characters a second) so that this is not a suitable terminal for large volumes of output, which are probably better produced on a line-printer in the batch-processing mode.

Many terminals have a paper-tape punch and reader attached to them. The terminal typewriter can be used to prepare paper tape instead of transmitting characters one by one to the computer. This tape can be transmitted to the computer via the paper-tape reader at your terminal at a much quicker speed than you can transmit it by typing, so that this mode of terminal usage is more economic. It is often advisable to make a paper-tape copy of a program.

You may be fortunate in using a *Visual Display Unit* (VDU) as your terminal. This usually comprises a typewriter keyboard, a cathode-ray display screen like a television set and a small local store in which input and output messages are collected. The user can visually check a complete message before transmission to the computer. When input is typed for transmission to the central computer a special character, known as a *cursor*, is used to indicate to the operator the position on the screen where the next input character will appear. The cursor is usually an underline or overline flashing symbol. One great advantage of the VDU is that it is noiseless. It is economical of computer time as compared with a typewriter terminal since a whole message is held in the store, so that it can be amended and edited, before it is transmitted as a unity to the computer. This is in contrast to the character-by-character transmission from the terminal typewriter or teletype. To assist editing, controls are provided to move the cursor in a vertical and horizontal direction so that it can be reset to the start of a line. The cursor invariably can be moved over existing data on the display screen without destroying it. The entry of new data at the position indicated by the cursor will overwrite existing data in that position.

Most displays provide facilities for erasure of a whole line and of the whole screen. Some have features of great assistance in editing messages, such as the insertion and deletion of characters and whole lines. Some displays can emphasise certain groups of characters by displaying them in double size, in italics or doubly bright.

The response time is much quicker with a VDU than with a typewriter terminal. Output speeds can attain 480 characters per second. There is a slight disadvantage as the terminal does not produce a hard-copy output record. There is considerable variation in the number of characters which a screen can display. One terminal displays 200 characters in 25 lines of 80 characters. The usual character set of the computer can be displayed. It is sometimes useful to have the computer generate headings on a display under which appropriate input data can be typed. On some displays it is ensured that such matter displayed by the com-

Aspects of Terminal Usage

puter is not treated as input. Graphs and drawings can also be displayed on the VDU.

The majority of computer peripherals such as card readers, line printers and graph plotters can be used as remote terminals to a computer used for remote batch-processing.

Special types of terminal have been designed for specific applications, such as the cash receipting terminal which incorporates a cash register which will give hard copy to receipt bills and a printed tally roll and also transmit the sums entered to the computer. Many data loggers can communicate directly with a remote computer.

A computer (often a small "mini-computer") can act as an "intelligent terminal" to another. A small computer can relieve the large remote central processor of many small tasks but can send data for large applications to the central computer and use the files attached to it. Since it can be programmed, it has greater versatility than the types of terminal discussed above which merely send input to and receive output from the central computer. Programs can be written to check the input before it is transmitted to the central computer.

Transmission Lines

If your terminal is on the same premises as the central computer it can be connected to it by a coaxial cable. This is a common method of connecting research laboratories with the central computer installation. There is however a constraint on the use of these links since they are limited to short distances.

For longer distances the Post Office data communication services, based on the existing telephone and telegraph networks, are used for data transmission to computers in Great Britain. Telex circuits, or telegraph private circuits, may be relevant to a user's needs when low-speed terminals such as teleprinters are used. The range of transmission speeds possible with these circuits is 45–100 bits (approximately 4.5 – 10 characters) per second. It is more common, however, to make the use of "dial-up" Post Office telephone lines. Lower-speed lines are available on the Post Office switched network which is routed through an exchange. It must be remembered that the Post Office system was primarily designed for the transmission of speech rather than data and that telephone exchanges were designed to serve telephone users who have a different pattern of usage to data transmission users. Higher transmission speeds are available on a privately leased line. Users of this facility can use the public switched network in the event of the failure of this fast line, although for that time the user would have to be content with reduced transmission rates.

Some of the individual Post Office services are:

Datel 200 provides transmission at speeds of up to 200 bits (20 characters) per second.
Datel 600 allows data transmission within the speed range of 600–1200 bits per second.
Datel 2400 allows transmission at the rate of 2400 bits per second but can only use private lines.

The Data Path from Terminal to Computer

The binary form in which data is represented when entering or leaving a computer is not suitable for transmission down telephone lines which were designed to carry signals generated by vocal patterns. The processes of conversion of binary data to voice frequencies are known as modulation and demodulation respectively. The device which performs these processes is known as a *modem*. Modems are naturally necessary at both the terminal and computer ends of a data transmission line.

Since modems are used to make a voice circuit carry data efficiently, the modulation technique is planned to adapt the waveform to the characteristics of the channel. The method of modulation must ensure that the maximum quantity of data is transmitted and should minimise the effects of distortion and noise.

The characteristics of a modem which gives optimum transmission on one type of telephone line may be relatively inefficient on another type of line. Lines passing through switching centres pick up more noise than is usually found on a private line. Any system which uses the Post Office telephone network must use the standard Post Office modems which sometimes require an adaptor to interface with the computer equipment of certain manufacturers.

To achieve maximum ultilisation of a leased line more than one terminal may be connected to a single line. Only one of these terminals can transmit at any one time but all can receive the same information. Since several terminals in such a situation may wish to transmit data

Aspects of Terminal Usage

simultaneously it is necessary for the computer to *poll* each terminal in turn or according to desired priorities.

With a great number of communication lines it would not be practicable to let the lines go straight into the computer. The interruptions from the terminals would be too frequent, so that the usual mode of working is for the communication lines to end in a device known as a *multiplexor*.

Multiplexors vary considerably in the number of lines which can be controlled and the amount of data which they can store. The chief work they perform, and which saves central processor time, is the assembly of bits into characters and messages, checking for transmission errors, and storing and queuing the messages received. The initiating of both the receipt of data from terminals and the transfer of output data from the central computer is performed by the multiplexor. Most multiplexors will deal with a great variety of types of terminal and line speeds. The multiplexor can transfer data to and from the central processor at a rate of many thousands of characters a second.

Some multiplexors are small computers with a program (which can be changed) for handling terminals and processing messages so that the central computer is freed from most of the tasks connected with the

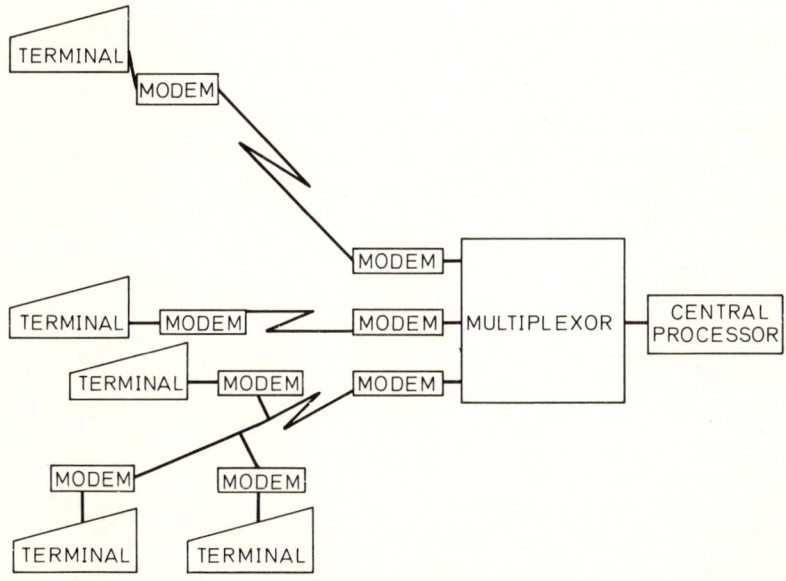

Figure 2.2 Data path from terminal to computer

handling of communication lines. This computer used to control communications lines is often known as a *front-end* processor. More flexibility can be attained by using a front-end processor in a complex network system where transmission requirements, such as the number of terminals and the priority of messages, change frequently.

Thus your terminal communicates with the computer via a modem, which translates binary information into voice frequencies, a transmission line which is terminated by another modem to re-convert the data into binary form, and a multiplexor to control the line and assemble the messages for transfer to and from the terminal (*Figure 2.2*).

A powerful computer with a store large enough to contain the necessary systems software and some current user programs and a backing store with capacity to take sections of many terminal programs not currently being activated is essential for a terminal system.

The hardware of the computer and communications system is only of utility when it is programmed. The next chapter will discuss the evolution and nature of the computer languages for ensuring that this complex and expensive system will perform the tasks you desire.

Chapter 3

PROGRAMMING LANGUAGES

It is desirable that the power and potential of the computer can be easily harnessed to applications by a form of instruction which is relevant to the application being programmed and which is symbolised in a notation familiar to practitioners of that application. The set of instructions which can be used on a computer is known as a computer language. Invariably many languages can be used on the same computer. Some like BASIC and FORTRAN are designed for the solution of scientific, technical and mathematical problems whilst the common computer language COBOL is designed for commercial data processing and file manipulation. There will also be, for a particular computer, languages designed for that particular computer rather than for a specific type of application.

All computers have an inbuilt instruction set designed round their hardware. This is known as machine code or machine language. These operate in binary. An early computer which had an instruction length of 20 bits (or binary digits) had each instruction entered by punching the requisite 20 ones or zeros in 4 rows of 5-channel paper tape. A one bit was represented by a punch; a zero by the absence of a punch. On one computer an instruction to clear location 8 of the store to zero could be entered on the binary keyboard as:

$$01011000000000001000$$

It was soon realised that the computer was versatile enough to be programmed to take input in a less outlandish form than the above and convert it to the necessary binary format. In the case of the foregoing instruction, the required function (or operation code) which occupies the first six bits was represented on the input tape as two digits between 0 and 7 (octal) and the last thirteen digits which represent the location of computer store affected by the operation was represented as a number between 0 and 8191, so that the above instruction would be punched as:

26 8

Most machine codes are written in some modified form such as the above rather than in the binary form which the computer hardware obeys. The program which translates the punched format into the machine code format is known as an assembler and is itself written in binary code. The number and power of machine code instructions vary considerably from one computer to another. Some reference more than one address or store location. Some computers have instructions to multiply, divide and compute mathematical functions, whilst on other computers only addition and subtraction can be performed by machine code instructions — other mathematical operations have to be supplied by the programmer. Machine code instructions are very detailed. On many computers the comparatively trivial operations of adding two numbers and storing the result will occupy three machine code instructions. Therefore a realistic program would occupy many instructions written in a form not meaningful to any person but the dedicated professional programmer. The format of many machine code instructions is complex and a detailed knowledge of machine code is lengthy to acquire. Since this code is built round the hardware of a computer the transfer of a program to a computer with different machine architecture would involve reprogramming. Machine code is very rarely used for the current generation of computers except by computer engineers. The majority of programs are written in a language which is translated or decoded by a computer program into machine code.

Assembly Languages (Low-level Languages)

These are close to machine code and are written for a particular computer. In the majority of cases each assembly language statement is translated into a single machine code instruction so that an assembly language program contains much of the detail which made machine code programs tedious to write.

The great advantage of an assembly language over machine code is that symbolic operation names and store names are used so that the program becomes slightly more meaningful to the writer. These symbols

Programming Languages

can often be mnemonic, so that a section of assembly language program to add two numbers and store the result could read:

> LDA PAY
> ADD TIP
> STA GPAY

Assembly languages usually contain statements known as macro-instructions or macros which generate several machine code instructions. These are common for input, output and file-handling purposes. Often the programmer is provided with the facility of writing his own macros. This is useful for common mathematical functions such as logarithms.

Programmers can work much faster in assembly language than in basic machine code and their error ratio is less. Since the assembly language bears a close relationship to the machine code of the computer for which it was designed there are no great difficulties in the computer translation of an assembly language program. However, assembly language is not a suitable medium for the scientist or research worker who wishes to write an occasional computer program. It takes too long for the non-professional programmer to learn and it contains too much detail.

High-level Computer Languages

An ideal computer language would use terms and notation relevant to the application area for which it was being used and would not be designed around the hardware of any individual computer. There are innumerable high-level computer languages which have some correspondence with these ideals.

The translating programs for such languages are naturally longer and more complicated than the equivalent programs to translate assembly languages. The translating program is known as a *compiler* and the process of translation is referred to as compilation. High-level language statements rarely have a one-to-one correspondence with machine code instructions. A typical high-level language statement in the common language BASIC could be:

> LET X = A+B/ (C−LOG (D+E) +SIN (F−G))

You can see that there is considerable resemblance to mathematical notation and that the statement is intelligible to others besides professional computer programmers.

Human languages such as English would be unsuitable as computer languages owing to the many semantic and syntactic ambiguities which can lurk even in such simple English sentences as:

and
"Time flies like an arrow."
"Julia has grown another foot this year."

and owing to the size and complexity of the vocabulary.

The common high-level languages which have been implemented for many computers are:

ALGOL 60
BASIC } for scientific and mathematical work
FORTRAN
COBOL   for commercial data processing
PL/I   for all types of computer application

The more complex the language, the more lengthy will be the process of compilation and the more space will the compiler occupy in the computer store. For interactive terminal usage it is desirable to have a language which compiles quickly so that there is little pause between the typing of statements and their translation into a machine code object program which will be obeyed. Thus the popular terminal language BASIC is less complex than ALGOL or PL/I because of the necessity of quick compilation in a terminal environment.

The ideal features of a programming language for the technical or scientific user who is essentially a "part-time" programmer are:

1. Adequacy to solve the majority of problems in relevant application areas without recourse to assembly language instructions to make up for deficiencies in the high-level computer language. Only BASIC of the common languages listed above contains comprehensive facilities for matrix arithmetic and manipulation. Many versions of ALGOL cannot deal with characters and symbols.

2. The symbols used in the language should be familiar and be present on the terminal typewriter keyboard. The full versions of ALGOL 60 and PL/I contain some exotic symbols such as logical operators.

3. The terms used in the language should be familiar to the user. In the case of the majority of terminal users a language similar to mathematical notation (like all the common languages except COBOL) would be satisfactory.

4. Since many terminal users are not going to be professional programmers the language should be easy to learn and use and not be intimately concerned with specialist features of computer hardware such as index registers and the internal representation of numbers and characters. The language should conceal the more intricate hardware features of a computer and circumvent any deficiencies so that a programmer will never realise that a particular computer does not in practice have a hardware divide facility.

5. The language should be independent of the hardware individualities or operating system of a specific computer so that programs can be readily transferred from one computer to another. Standard versions of FORTRAN and COBOL sponsored by the American National Standards Institution have been recently implemented for many computers in common use. There are however many "dialects" of common computer languages including BASIC in existence which extend the scope of the languages or enable them to utilise the hardware excellencies of a specific computer but which have the disadvantage of limiting the use of programs using these extensions to a single type of computer.

6. The language should be rigorously defined so that all writers or compilers will interpret the facilities of the language in the same way. A simple English definition of a language would inevitably introduce considerable ambiguities, so it is usually defined in a formal manner. (For a detailed definition of a programming language using meta-linguistic techniques, interested readers are referred to the ALGOL Report published in the Communications of the Association for Computing Machinery, January 1963, pp. 1–17.) Working definitions of the syntax of the major computer languages have been in existence for some time. It is essential for users that the same statement in a computer language should not be interpreted differently on different types of computer.

7. The language should have efficient compilers implemented for computers in common use.

In addition to these general features there are certain facilities which assist the speedy writing of programs which the majority of programming languages designed for scientific and technical work contain. The facilities which are of greatest assistance to programmers are:

1. Data names with some mnemonic element can be used. In the BASIC language a programmer is restricted to only one alphabetic character (and a numeric symbol) in a data name. Yet this can make programs more meaningful than the use of absolute or relative addresses of the computer store which is necessary in some low-level computer languages. The other common high-level languages allow greater freedom to the programmer in his choice of data names than BASIC so that variables with names such as PAY and MEAN can be used.

2. Various types of data such as numbers, characters and arrays of various dimensions can be declared.

3. Arithmetic expressions of the complexity of the examples on page 69 can be written and standard mathematical functions such as LOG and COS are supplied.

4. Conditional statements are supplied which are one of the most essential features of computing. The programmer using these has power to make a test on the data inside the computer and obey a specific branch as a result of the test. A straightforward example of this could be the ALGOL statement:

<u>if</u> X = Zero <u>then</u> write text "ZERO"; <u>else</u> write text "NOTZERO";

5. Most computer programs obey the same sequences of statements over and over again. A payroll program for 1000 employees has the essential parts of the program repeated 1000 times and many mathematical programs involve repeated iteration of the same sequence of computer statements. Parts of a program which it is desired to repeat many times are known as loops and high-level languages contain facilities to control loops and ensure they are obeyed the required number of times.

6. High-level computer languages allow independent sections of a program to be written in such a way that they can be transferred from one program to another. These sections are known as subroutines and many programs consist of a series of subroutines written by separate programmers since they can be written independently of any program using them. A typical subroutine would be a sequence of statements to calculate the mean and standard deviation of input items which would be useful in many statistical applications. Subroutines can also be used within a single program for sequences of statements which you need to repeat at various points in the program.

The development of high-level languages has been a boon to the user who has not the time or inclination to master the intricacies of assembly languages. Yet it is inadvisable to rush into writing statements for any program except the most simple without careful planning of the method of computation. Hastily written programs invariably require a great deal of testing and development since it is likely that they will contain major errors and will omit initially some important stages in the computational process. The next chapter will discuss the various stages in the planning, writing and testing of a program.

Chapter 4

STAGES IN WRITING AND TESTING A PROGRAM

You should ensure that there is not a program in existence, and that could be made available to you with a minimum of difficulty, which performs essentially the same task as your proposed program. Much valuable time can be wasted by "re-inventing the wheel". Most installations have a list of available programs, and other valuable sources of programs are the computer manufacturers and time-sharing computer service bureaux. There is not the extensive library of BASIC programs available which can be found in FORTRAN but there are many available programs for mathematical, statistical and engineering applications. If you wish to program a common application in these application areas (such as curve fitting) it is likely that a suitable program can be easily made available for your use.

Any suitable program should have copious and relevant documentation so that you can see the input and output formats, the computational methods used, any limitations, the error conditions catered for and the form of error messages which are output. Such documentation will enable you to ascertain if the program really will be an acceptable substitute. Only experienced programmers should attempt emendation and alteration of such a program since one single statement replaced may imply many other alterations which would not be obvious to a beginner.

If you find that there is no suitable alternative to the writing of your own program it is as well to make detailed plans before the writing of the statements which you will enter at the typewriter terminal. Careful thought in the preliminary stages of program creation will save a great deal of frustration when the program is put to the test of running at the terminal.

The first step in planning a program is the precise definition of the problem for which a computer solution is desired. This definition is

Stages in Writing and Testing a Program

fairly obvious in the exercises to the later chapters in this book. In many situations, however, the initial definition of the problem may omit such important factors as the extent to which input should be verified by the program itself (in terminal work it is easy for a novice to key in erroneous digits), the exact format of the typewriter output desired and the procedures to be taken in case of various types of error. If others in addition to yourself are going to make use of your program it is as well to define and include in the documentation any cases for which the program will not be designed to cater. If you were writing a simple program to calculate means of numbers input at the terminal typewriter you would have to decide on any upper limit to the number of elements with which you intended to deal and the action you would take if only one element was input.

When the problem has been rigorously defined the next stage is the consideration of possible methods of solution. In numerical analysis there are often alternative methods of evaluation which you should consider. A method of solving a problem which can be transferred to a computer for reasons of speed and accuracy is often referred to as an *algorithm*. You may find help in the algorithms published in Computer Journal and the Communications of the Association for Computing Machinery. Even though the majority of these programs are in ALGOL they are well documented as regards the computational method involved.

The choice of algorithm should naturally be conditioned by your ability and experience in programming and by the facilities at your disposal in the computer language you are using. BASIC is particularly suitable for algorithms involving matrix manipulation since alone of the common computer languages it can invert a matrix in a single program statement. In some cases the computer system you propose to use has some relevance to the method chosen as some problems are not very appropriate to solution at a terminal.

After a method has been chosen the problem must be analysed for computer solution. Often a rough written series of verbal steps is the first stage in the translation of the problem into programming terms. A program, using a looping technique, to read 10 numbers input at the typewriter and calculate and print the mean could be initially represented as:

1. Clear total
2. Clear count

3. Read a number
4. Add number to total
5. Add 1 to count
6. If count <10 go to step 3
7. If not; compute and print mean.

These steps are easier to alter in the case of a logical error than a series of statements in a programming language. In a more complicated problem than the above the verbal visualisation usually begins with broad steps and then translates each of these into greater detail. The logic of the process is checked for faults at each stage.

Intending programmers should aim to visualise problems in terms of loops wherever possible so that the same sequence of statements, often controlled by a count, is used repeatedly. The algorithm for reading 10 numbers shown above is more elegant and suited to the capabilities of the computer than the linear method which would appear as:

Clear total
Read a number and add to total
Read a number and add to total
....
Read 10th number and add to total
etc.

The general concept of a loop for processing a known number of items can be represented as:

1. Clear count
2. Perform process
3. Augment count by 1
4. If count less than terminal value go to step 2
5. (Exit from loop).

Flowcharts

It is conventional to represent the steps in the solution of a program in a graphic form after the preliminary verbal process described above.

Such a graph is known as a flowchart. These should be drawn for all programs except the most trivial and are especially useful in a program

Stages in Writing and Testing a Program

which contains many branches since the various loops and their points of return to the main program are clearly indicated. There is a tendency to omit flowcharting and proceed immediately to the coding of a program in a computer language. This attitude can lead to considerable waste of valuable computer time since a complex program without a flowchart nearly always contains errors which a flowchart would have highlighted. A flowchart is also useful when used in conjunction with the program itself to ascertain faults which have been found during program testing. It is imperative that any emendations made to the program during this testing phase are incorporated in the flowchart. Flowcharts are vital if your program is to be used by others since they are more immediately understood than a mass of coded program statements.

Each step in a flowchart is written in a box; different shapes of boxes are used for various purposes and most computer manufacturers supply templates for the drawing of these boxes, containing an explanation of the significance of each shape. The shape of flowchart boxes has been standardised (BS 4058). The majority of the shapes are used for systems design rather than programming. Only two boxes are normally necessary: a rectangular box for a computational step and a diamond-shaped box for a comparison or decision.

There are computer programs which will create flowcharts from statements in certain computer languages. These are useful for obtaining a final flowchart from a fully tested program or for obtaining one after such a program has been amended, but they are naturally no substitute for the flowchart which is preliminary to the writing of the program.

The boxes in a flowchart can be used for any desired level of detail. In a complicated or lengthy program there are often two flowcharts. The first is in broad detail and the second descends to the level of a statement in a programming language in each box. References can be used to link the two flowcharts. Box 1 in the first flowchart could originate boxes 1,1,1,2, etc., in the more detailed one.

The flowchart of *Figure 4.1* shows the iterative process of obtaining a square root (s) of an input number (n) which is shown as a BASIC program on page 79. This uses the formula:

$$s = \tfrac{1}{2}(x+n/x)$$

where x is the previous s and continues the iteration until the difference between two successive iterations is less than 10^{-6}. x is given an initial value of 1. It will be seen that this flowchart uses descriptive terms

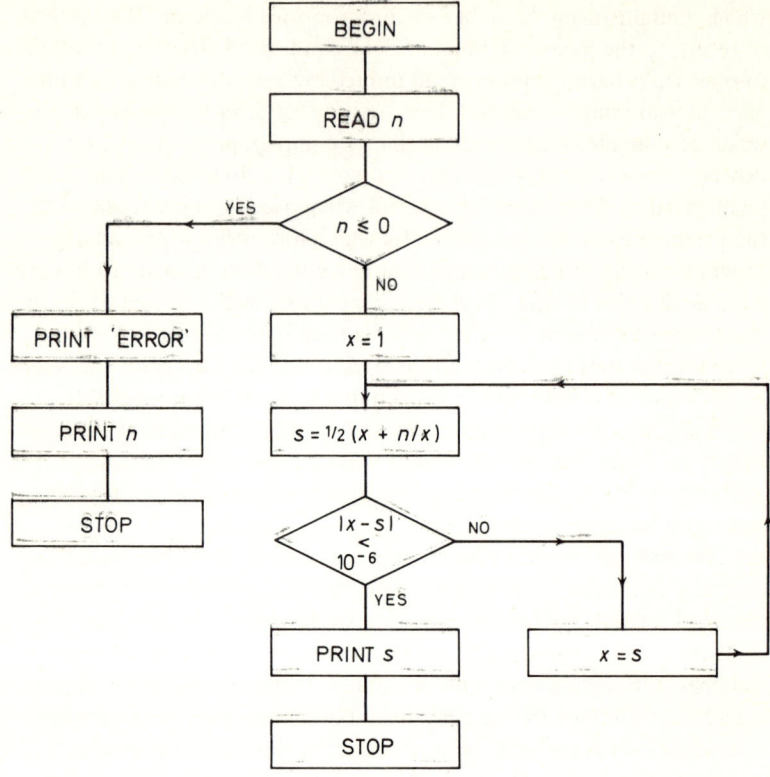

Figure 4.1 Flowchart of the iterative process of obtaining a square root (s) of an input number (n)

rather than the programming language statements on page 79. A subroutine which you have not written is represented on your flowchart by its name inside a single box. If you have written it yourself it is represented in the main program in the above manner and the flowchart(s) of the subroutine will be drawn on a separate sheet.

Checking of Flowcharts

Wherever possible all the flowcharts for your program should be checked for error by another person with a knowledge of the problem you are trying to solve. Potential programmers invariably become enamoured of their own creation so that they are often blind to logical faults. The best way to check a flowchart is to work through it step by step with small amounts of data similar to that which will be encountered in the actual operational program and to ascertain if the results at each stage are what would be expected. The error branches of the program should be tested as well.

The use of a hand-calculator is necessary in the checking of many flowcharts and programs in order to be certain of accurate computation upon the test data.

This checking process may reveal some error conditions for which you have not catered and which have been noticed by the programmer checking the program. You should be on your guard against too meticulous program checks for input errors, whether the input is to be included in the program (BASIC DATA statement), inserted at the typewriter terminal or punched. In the last case the input will have invariably been subjected to a verification process after the punching. With regard to insertion of data, in many cases you will be typing in the data yourself and not visualising making your elementary efforts available for common use. Even in this situation, however, you should make provision for that fact that you may make errors in typing input at the terminal typewriter, but should not take over-excessive precautions.

The checking should confirm that you have used appropriate input and output formats. If you are using punched input you should have made certain that the input is easy to punch and, if there are large volumes of input, which is common in some statistical programs, you should consult with the punch room as to the best format. If input is to be entered at the terminal it is as well to insert program instructions to type a reminder to yourself (or whoever is using the program at the typewriter terminal) of the form and range of the numerical data to be inserted during the running of the program.

For scientific work it is unlikely that you will be using any pre-printed stationery for your output so that it is imperative that you should provide headings to the columns and any verbal description which may be appropriate. Textual explanations are easy to program in high-level computer languages and even if the results are solely for your own use and edification you should from your first program onwards aim at producing more than a barren string of numerals. If you are printing a great deal of output at the typewriter you will have to decide on how many lines you wish to form a reasonable page on the continuous stationery and insert appropriate program instructions to produce your desired pagination. If you are producing your results for a visual display screen you will have to ensure that your output is divided into units suitable for the constraints created by the dimensions of the screen.

Coding the Program

When the desk-checking or "dry-running" of the flowchart is concluded the program is then coded in statements of the chosen programming language ready for running at the terminal. High-level languages are essentially formal and careful attention should be paid to detail in writing your program. Care should be taken especially with punctuation (e.g. the separation of items in a BASIC PRINT statement by commas), proper correspondence of opening and closing brackets, and with using the exact form of expression as described in the relevant programming text. You should see that enough comment (BASIC REMARKS) is included in your program to ensure that you will understand your mental processes in six months' time. You should also incorporate any temporary print statements which may be necessary in tracing the progress of the program while it is under development. These are described in greater detail on page 41.

If possible, the coding should be checked by another person with knowledge of the programming language you are using. This checking will use the flowchart and the documented results of the checking of the flowchart since the checking of the logic of the program will have been done. The main purpose of the checking of the coding is to ensure that the flowchart boxes have been accurately translated into programming language terminology. If the program is written in BASIC the statement numbers which must preface each statement should be written on the appropriate box of the detailed flowchart to make correspondence easy to see. The checking should theoretically ensure that elementary programming mistakes such as the omission of a bracket or punctuation symbol and confusion with variable names are detected.

Program Testing and Development

When the program is first run at the terminal it is not likely it will work unless it is a relatively simple one. This is not an unduly pessimistic assumption or one which belittles your mental powers, as even the most

Stages in Writing and Testing a Program

experienced programmers find their initial efforts are not proof against the remorseless logic of the computer. The process of testing and correcting a program until it is in an operational state is sometimes known as checking-out or (inelegantly) as debugging. Computer time is expensive and the correction of errors at this stage is frustrating and sometimes difficult, so that careful checking of the flowchart and program before it is run will minimise the amount of time used for the program testing phase. There are three types of fault which become apparent during this stage in the development of a program.

1. "Grammatical" errors which are detected by the compiler so that the program will not be compiled. Compilers print the reason for the refusal to compile. Sometimes an error number will be printed at your terminal so that you will have to look up the corresponding error message in the manual. If the compiler at the installation you are using is of this type you will need the manual by you at the terminal. Other compilers will print a message indicative of the error and show why the statement is wrong. The majority of error numbers and messages are typed immediately after the entry of an erroneous line. In some cases, however, an error indication cannot be given until the end of the program. Common errors which prevent a program from compiling are:

    Incorrect punctuation.
    A referred-to line number has not been found.
    Unrecognisable word or statement type.
    Incorrect form of statement.

2. Execution errors which are detected during the running of the program. These errors attempt to instruct the computer to perform an impossible task. Common execution errors, which are revealed by error messages printed at the terminal are:

    Division by zero.
    Reading a number beyond data specification.
    Attempting to extract the square root or logarithm of a negative number.
    The result of an arithmetic expression is too large for the computer.
    Program or array too large.

3. Execution errors which do not give rise to system error messages but which either produce a completely erroneous answer to the problem or produce an infinite loop which has to be ended at the terminal typewriter. These are undetected errors in the logic of your program and are often the most difficult to detect.

Program testing should be performed with small amounts of data analagous to the test data used in checking the flowchart. If a loop is to be obeyed 1000 times, testing should be done with five items. Program testing should cater for all the error branches as well as the normal paths through the program. The answers to the processing of test data should be known so that any discrepancies can be identified immediately.

If the program divides into many branches you will need to design tests which will be used in more than one test run of the program. Several tests will have to be made of such a program, where each trial tests a certain number of branches. Often the trial data used in testing the flowchart can be used here.

A long program can be divided into subroutines for easy testing and when all these are satisfactorily operational they can be run in combination. This technique has been applied extensively to data processing programs and in that environment is often termed "modular programming".

Testing should be done in short, sharp bursts. Elementary grammatical errors can be corrected at the terminal typewriter but other types of error can rarely be corrected without taking the program away from the terminal and studying it closely with the flowchart.

Aids to Program Testing

Some programming languages have extensive diagnostic features whereby the changing contents of certain variables can be printed out during the execution of the program. This can be a great help during the testing of a program. Other types of trace facilities print out statement numbers each time the normal sequence of program flow is affected by a conditional statement, so that the path a program actually takes is clearly indicated. It is often possible to get a print-out of the relevant part of the store (called a dump) when a program fails but as this dump will be in some sort of coded binary or octal notation it may not be a great deal of help to you.

Some versions of BASIC do not possess the above facilities but you can insert suitable variants for yourself. PRINT statements can be inserted so that you can see how certain variable values change in the course of the program. If your program uses repeated loops you may only wish to print out these values the first and last time a loop is obeyed, so that you will have to write a small subroutine to accomplish this. You can trace the program path by printing out the statement number after an IF statement. These extra print statements which you insert purely for program testing should not be too numerous. Only items should be printed which can be of real assistance in revealing why the program has lapsed into error after searching examination of the flowchart has not revealed any reason to you. Such statements inserted for testing purposes need not be added to the flowcharts. You should be sure to take them out of the program when the testing is satisfactorily completed since the extra printing will be time consuming and irrelevant to the purpose of the program.

Many commercial data processing programs are part of a suite of programs whereby the output from one program often forms the input for the next program in the suite. This interconnection between programs is rare in technical applications although it sometimes occurs with statistical operations. If your program is part of such a suite the programs have to be tested in conjunction as well as individually to ensure that information is passed between them in the expected form. The results should be kept of the final tests which show that the main branches of the program are working correctly. A box-file forms ideal storage for flowcharts, flowchart checking sheets, program coding and test results.

Documentation

Even if the program is not going to be used by others there should be some documentation so that if you have occasion to use it again you will have more than lines of coding to refresh your memory. Much relevant documentation has been mentioned at the end of the previous section where it was suggested that the chief items should be kept in a box-file.

The standard and extent of required documentation may be determined by your installation although interactive technical programs do not need the detail which is required of commercial file-processing program suites. Whatever documentation is kept it is essential that amendments to operational programs are recorded in the flowcharts and coding of the master set. Other items which could prove useful in the documentation of terminal programs are operating procedures, error conditions and messages, input and output formats and limitations, and a brief note on method used if the program is concerned with numerical analysis. If the program is meant for batch-processing rather than terminal working you will need to provide detailed instructions to the computer operators and the action they are to take at various stages in the program when you arrange that a message is displayed for them.

Chapter 5

INTRODUCTION TO THE BASIC LANGUAGE

BASIC is an acronym for Beginners All-purpose Symbolic Instruction Code and was developed at Dartmouth College, New Hampshire by Professors J. G. Kemeny and T. E. Kurtz under the terms of a grant from the National Science Foundation. It was first implemented in 1965 on a GE 225 computer and was designed as a simple language for a time-sharing environment. It was primarily intended as a medium for the solution of numerical problems although extensions have been added which permit character manipulation.

Paramount in the design of the language was ease in learning and usage for the non-professional programmer, such as the statistician or engineer, wishing to use computer terminal facilities. Compilation time is speedy and the resulting object program is efficient. BASIC has been implemented on the majority of computers which you are likely to encounter and is the most widely used computer language designed primarily for interactive working.

Even though the language is easy to master it contains useful features such as the matrix instructions not found in FORTRAN or ALGOL. It also contains the great majority of facilities which are found in any high-level computer language designed for numerical work.

The development of BASIC for computers other than the GE range has led to a series of extensions and the creation of numerous dialects of BASIC. Some variations are described in Chapter 12. This book is chiefly concerned with the common core of BASIC which is found in all implementations and which is more than adequate for the purposes for which the language was designed. Care should be taken in using any of the non-standard features (such as the FILE facilities) as these differ considerably and you will have to make considerable amendments to certain sections of your program if you transfer your work from one computer to another.

Although it was originally designed for a terminal typewriter, the powerful simplicity of BASIC has led to its implementation for other forms of input such as punched cards and punched paper tape and to its use in a batch-processing environment. The following chapters assume that you are using BASIC at a typewriter terminal although the statements of the language are in no way different if you are using a less direct form of input to the computer system.

The differences which arise if you are using BASIC in a batch-processing environment are concerned with certain system commands which will be mentioned in the programming manual for the computer you are using. If you are punching statements on tape or cards the next section describing entry of a BASIC program at a terminal typewriter will naturally be inapplicable to your requirements. All the rest of the facilities of BASIC are equally valid to all forms of input.

Initial Steps in Entering a BASIC Program at a Terminal Typewriter

The usual first step if the Post Office network is used is to dial the number of the computer so that a connection with the computer is established (in Britain on receipt of the dialling tone the DATA button on the telephone receiver is depressed unless there is an equivalent key on the typewriter).

The computer system now asks various questions to establish your authenticity and outputs various pieces of information. The exact procedure varies with various types of computer and in various installations. Common items of information which you may be expected to supply are:

1. User number — used for accounting and security purposes. Sometimes a complex password system is invoked here.
2. Project identifier — here you supply an identifier for your own reference purposes.
3. Language — here you will type BASIC. Sometimes the actual word the computer types for this language response is SYSTEM.
4. You may be then asked if you wish to use a former program or write a new one. Your responses are OLD or NEW. In this case when you are entering a BASIC program you will type NEW.

Introduction to the BASIC Language 45

5. You are then asked to supply a program (often referred to as FILE) name. Rules for names vary from one installation to another. It is worth emphasising that, in some systems, spaces are important so that TASK 1 and TASK1 would be regarded as separate programs.
6. Usually after your insertion of the program name the terminal will respond with READY. You can now commence typing the program proper on the terminal typewriter.

A typical printout of this initial dialogue between user and terminal could be:

(underlined words are typed by the computer)

<u>ON AT 14.30 05/17/69</u>
<u>BEGIN SESSION</u>
MAKE JULIA BASIC
<u>FILE:JULIA   TYPE BASIC   CREATED</u>
<u>OK</u>

(then you type your program).

You should familiarise yourself with the signing-on procedure of the installation you use so that you can quickly enter the system and commence productive computer usage. If you make a mistake the computer will invariably retype the question, except in the case of a mistyped, invalid user number or password when you may probably be cut off completely for security reasons.

The computer signing-on sequence is language independent (in some systems you could have typed FORTRAN as the language instead of BASIC). It is essential to differentiate between BASIC proper and this initial procedure which has considerable minor variations from one installation to another.

In the majority of installations the signing-on procedure will incorporate the request NEW or OLD. Your reply to this (NEW) is an example of a system command. These commands are again independent of programming language and are addressed to the operating system to cause it to handle programs or program statements in various ways. The function and repertoire of system commands differ between installations but in view of their potential value to you it is to your interest to consult the appropriate manual to ascertain what system commands are available for your use. Below are listed some common system commands the equivalents of which are usually found and which will be useful to you.

> RUN — causes the program you have typed or requested to be executed.
> SAVE — if this is typed at the end of the program, the program will be stored on file so that it can be retrieved on subsequent occasions by typing OLD and the program name.
> UNSAVE — this will take a stored program from file when you have no further use for it.
> RENAME — this allows you to change the name of the current program, which itself remains unchanged. You will be asked to type a new name on the terminal typewriter.
> CATALOG — this provides a list of program names currently on your file. It is an useful system command if you are apprehensive of duplicating a program name.

Correction of Typing Errors

Even the most experienced programmer sometimes has "finger trouble" at a terminal typewriter. A common way to correct an error is to retype the whole line. If two statements are prefaced with the same number or *line number* the computer accepts the second and ignores the first statement. For instance, in the following sequence of statements:

```
30   LET B = 7
40   PRINT A,B,A,+ B, A − B
40   PRINT A,B,A + B, A − B
```

the corrected statement 40 replaces the incorrect one.

A Simple Program

This is a very trivial program which prints two numbers, their sum and their difference, but illustrates some important points about the BASIC language. Some important elementary features appearing in lines of this program will be described as they are vital to any program in the language.

Introduction to the BASIC Language

```
   10    REM A SIMPLE PROGRAM
   20    LET A = 4
   30    LET B = 7
   40    PRINT A,B,A + B, B − A
99999    END
```

It should be reasonably clear what this program performs. The values of 4 and 7 are put in store locations of the computer which are referred to as A and B, and the values of the numbers, their sum and their difference are printed.

If you are at the terminal and you type in this program followed by the system command RUN on a line by itself, the program will be executed. Your results will appear in a form like:

4   7   11   3

and will be followed by some information about the execution of the program itself which varies from one computer to another.

Now you can try some program basically like the example above. You can use any letters for variable names but at the moment you must confine your arithmetic to addition and subtraction. You must *not* let your statements be longer than a single line. Try more than two variables and negative numbers. You will be able to get some useful practice in familiarising yourself with the terminal. Some of the important BASIC rules which you have encountered in this elementary program will now be described.

Line Numbers

As opposed to system commands, each BASIC program statement must have a line number between 1 and (commonly) 99999. There is variation in various systems between the maximum integer allowed for a line number. At least one space must be left between the line number and the statement following it. Leading zeros (e.g. 007) may be typed as a line number but usually no blank spaces or other characters must appear when the line number is typed.

Each line number must be unique within a program. If two lines have the same number the first line with the number is ignored on compilation. You will remember that this facility is used to correct an erroneous line by retyping the correct statement with the same line number as the statement which was in error.

The program is automatically arranged during compilation in order of line number so that if a line is unintentionally omitted it can be inserted at a later point in the program, e.g.

```
50  PRINT B + J
99  END
60  PRINT J − B
RUN
```

The above program will now print the difference of the variables immediately after their sum.

If you become confused in a long program in which you have inserted many corrections and lines out of order, there is a useful system command LIST which will type out the current program in line number order.

It is usual to leave gaps between line numbers rather than use consecutive integers, so that subsequent insertions can easily be made. It will be observed that all the above examples commonly use multiples of 10 for line numbers. END is always the last line of the program and is often given the maximum line number allowed by the system so that insertion of substantial sections of program can be made if necessary.

General Format of a BASIC Statement

There is some variation in the number of characters allowed on a line — the usual number is 75. Since line numbers are unique, each statement must not occupy more than a single line. It is possible already for you to visualise some print statements containing many variables and their combination by plus and minus signs. If they are longer than the permitted number of characters per statement they will have to be written as two separate statements with different line numbers.

Blanks or spaces can be allowed within a statement so that you can space your line as you wish.

```
170  LETL    = 23
170  LET L   = 23
170  L ET L = 2   3
```

are all acceptable (if slightly eccentric) ways of writing the same statement. (The only exception to the rule of the disregard of spaces within

Introduction to the BASIC Language

a statement is in an alphanumeric literal which will be discussed in Chapter 10.)

You may find it convenient to indent certain lines or statements of your program for emphasis.

Now that the general form of a BASIC statement has been examined it is appropriate to examine the individual commands used in the sample program.

Remarks

```
10    REM A SIMPLE PROGRAM
```

The command REM introduces a comment meant to explain the program to a reader and is ignored by the compiler. This is useful if it is likely that your program will be used by others at some future time when you will not be available to explain its sophistications. It will also be of utility to you if you return to a rarely used program you have written after some lapse of time. It must be remembered that the REM statement, although not executed, requires a line number. It is useful to include in REM statements at the head of a program the date of writing, any pertinent observations on the method used and the name of the author.

```
10    REM PROGRAM LORETTA WRITTEN BY
20    REM JULIA ALISON SANDERSON
30    REM 13 APRIL 1972
40    REM IT CASTS HOROSCOPES
50    REM BIRTHDAY IN D, TIME (GREENWICH M.T.) IN T
60    REM MONTH, IN M, YEAR IN Y
```

LET Statement

```
20    LET A = 4
30    LET B = 7
```

The LET statement assigns the value of the expression on the right hand of = to the part of computer store referred to throughout a program by the variable name on the left-hand side. The previous contents of the variable are overwritten and lost: thus great care must be taken by a beginner to have clear identification of what each variable contains so that valuable data is not overwritten. The use of the REM statement can assist you to identify readily what important variables contain.

Some systems such as the IBM Call/360 set all variables to the value of zero at the start of a program. Your own programming manual will tell you if your compiler has adopted this practice. If you are likely to use various different computers it is as well to make no assumption about the initial value of variables and none will be made in this book.

The form of the assignment statement is:

$$\text{LET variable} = \begin{cases} \text{arithmetic expression} \\ \text{value in another variable} \\ \text{constant} \end{cases}$$

Only the third type of assignment statement has been used in the sample program. The first type of assignment statement will be discussed in the next chapter. This chapter will deal with the rules for variable names and numeric constants.

Variable Names

Variable names are restricted to the 26 letters of the alphabet and to these letters followed by one of the 10 digits 0–9. (The use of a digit does not mean that the variable is subscripted. The rules for arrays will be defined in Chapter 8.) Thus legal variables could be A,U,Z,J6,Q0,P3,H9. The names TAX, P14, £d, ABC are illegal.

In writing programs for someone other than yourself to type into a terminal it is often as well to avoid the variables such as O, S and Z, which could (if written by hand) be confused with digits. There are 286 allowed variable names in BASIC so that there will always be sufficient for your requirements without recourse to those composed of symbols which could be misinterpreted.

We have already seen how numerical values can be stored in a variable. The LET statement also allows the value of one variable to be stored in another, e.g.

```
900    LET R = 65
910    LET V = R
```

The above statements put 65 in both R and V. The value of R is unchanged when it is placed in V. When drawing the flowchart it is as well to assign variables to the quantities so that after a lapse of time you

Introduction to the BASIC Language

can identify what you have stored in G8. The judicious use of the REM facility can also assist in identifying important variables, but too much verbosity in remarks should be deprecated.

Numeric Constants

A numeric constant is used to insert a definite numeric value in a variable. These can occur singly:

    30   LET B = 7

or in expressions, e.g.

    80   LET L = 17 + P

The detailed form of arithmetic expressions will be described in the next chapter.

There are three ways of expressing numeric constants in BASIC.

1. *Integers.* These can be signed or unsigned and leading zeros are ignored. Each system has a limitation on the number of digits (usually nine) allowed. Commas within a constant are not permitted so that 81,000 would be an illegal constant.

Valid integer constants would be:

$$17, -7892, 0, 007, -015, +213$$

2. *Real Numbers.* These have a decimal point and usually a fractional part. The above remarks about signs, leading zeros, prohibition of embedded commas and maximum number of digits apply to constants in this form. The whole-number part can be omitted in a fraction.

Valid real constants would be:

$$1.5678, +0.876, -4.0, .876, -.85400085, 0.023$$

3. *Exponential Numbers.* This form is normally used for expressing very large and very small numbers which would contain too many digits to express in the ways described above. Every computer has limitations upon the range of numbers which can be represented and you should familiarise yourself with these.

The form for exponential numeric constants is:

    Mantissa E exponent (power of 10)

so that:

$$19.2E-2$$

would represent 0.192.

Each part of the number may be signed and contain leading zeros. The exponent must be an integer of not more than two digits. The exact maximum value of the exponent will vary with the computer used and details will be available in the appropriate programming manual. The number 123 can be represented in various exponential forms as:

```
           12.3E+1
           +1.23E2
           .123E03
           123.E0
           1230E-1
           .0000000123E10
```

Simple Printing

```
    40   PRINT A,B,A+B, B-A
```

More sophisticated printing than that discussed below will be described in later chapters. We can think of the PRINT statement at the moment as being of the form:

PRINT (list of expressions)

In most cases the printing will be done on the terminal typewriter. Expressions can include constants as well as variables but must be accommodated in a single line. Otherwise a multiple print statement will be required. An expression can be a single variable or constant. The sample program could be sufficiently rewritten as:

```
    10   REM A SIMPLE PROGRAM
    20   PRINT 7,4,7+4,7-4
 99999   END
```

since constants as well as variables can appear in arithmetic expressions inside a PRINT statement.

In the majority of versions of BASIC the length of line on the terminal typewriter is considered to be 75 characters and the line is divided into 5 "fields" of 15 characters. If (as in the example above) a comma is used to separate the values to be printed, each value will be printed in a separate field or zone. The exact positioning of the number within the zone varies with different computer systems. Typical output from the above PRINT statement could be:

7   4   11   3

If more than 5 zones are needed for a PRINT statement the values are printed on the next line or lines. Different versions of the language will print different numbers of significant digits. Printing is done in the E format in some versions of BASIC if the number is too large or too small to be contained in the number of significant digits provided. One version will print 421360271 as .421360E+9 and .00000017 as .17E−6.

If it was desired to print each expression in the PRINT statement of the sample program on a separate line individual PRINT statements would be used for each item in the existing PRINT list, e.g.

```
40   PRINT A
50   PRINT B
60   PRINT A + B
70   PRINT B − A
```

The statement without a list:

```
10   PRINT
```

would skip a line and is sometimes useful for vertical spacing of output on the typewriter. The following section of program:

```
170   PRINT 17
180   PRINT
190   PRINT 5
200   PRINT
210   PRINT 1969
```

would type out as:

17

5

1969

It should be remembered that the expressions in a PRINT statement must be separated from one another. The statement:

    890   PRINT A B N+M

is incorrect and should be rewritten as:

    890   PRINT A,B,N+M

The above features of the PRINT statement will be ample for your present needs although the PRINT statement is capable of considerable variety in formatting the output. These more elegant alternatives will be described later in this book.

Exercises 5.1

1. Using two variables, write a program to print the values of 1017, 43, 1017 + 86, 2034, − 974.

2. Rewrite the following program correctly:

   ```
   10   LET X0 = 19
        LET Y = 7
   40   LET A10 = −6
   50   LET 8 = B
   60   PRINT X0 Y Y + B
   70   PRINT,
   90   PRINT A10 + X0
   80   END
   ```

3. Assign values to A and B and use as few instructions as possible to print the values of 2A + 3B (without looking ahead and using the multiply instruction!).

4. Rewrite the above program to print A,B and 2A + 3B on separate lines with a blank line after each number.

5. Interchange values which you store in A and Z and print on separate lines the original contents and exchanged contents of variables A and Z.

Chapter 6

HOW TO WRITE SIMPLE ARITHMETICAL PROGRAMS IN BASIC

Arithmetic Expressions

Only addition and subtraction have been encountered so far. You will remember that the PRINT statement of the sample program in Chapter 5 included both addition and subtraction:

    40   PRINT A,B,A + B,B − A

In the above example the values of B − A and A + B would be lost after the execution of the PRINT statement and if they were required again they would have to be recomputed. To avoid perpetual recalculation of more complicated arithmetic expressions it is more usual to use an arithmetic expression at the right-hand side of an assignment statement where variables and constants can be mixed. Some typical elementary arithmetic expressions in assignment statements would be:

    210   LET Y = X + 7
    220   LET I = 18 − D
    230   LET Q = V − L + H
    240   LET Z = 190 + C − F + T

A common BASIC statement when using a count of the number of times a section of program is performed is:

    670   LET K = K + 1

Although this appears algebraic lunacy it merely increases the existing value of K by 1. Naturally the old value of K is lost. You will remember this type of statement in the flowchart on page 34. The arithmetic operators for operations other than addition and subtraction are given below.

* Multiply
/ Divide
↑ raise to a power (exponentiate)

The exponentiate symbol is sometimes written as **. Variables and constants can be combined by the above operators to form arithmetic expressions, e.g.

    800   LET D = Y↑3 + 4.5*X − 3   ($d = y^3 + 4.5x - 3$)
    810   LET E = 4*A*C   ($e = 4ac$)
    820   LET L = A/2   ($l = a/2$)
    830   LET R = 192 − P↑1.5 + F   ($r = 192 - p^{1.5} + f$)

It is important (even for experienced programmers) to remember that operators (especially *) are never implicit and must always be written. Therefore 8.9P and 6AB are incorrect in a BASIC arithmetic expression and should be rewritten as:

$$8.9*P \quad \text{and} \quad 6*A*B$$

It should be noted also that a minus sign coming before a variable is treated as a subtraction sign rather than a negation:

−3↑2 would be evaluated as -9 ($-(3^2)$), rather than $+9$ (-3^2).

The value of an arithmetic expression is computed to the number of digits of accuracy of the particular computer system, which can be ascertained from the appropriate manufacturer's manual. There can also be found the range of numbers which can be represented. Usually a diagnostic message is typed during the execution of a program if the evaluation of an arithmetic expression leads to a number too large (overflow) or too small (underflow) to be represented on the particular computer.

There are certain rules in the formation of BASIC expressions which differ from the construction of algebraic expressions and which may cause confusion to a beginner.

1. Two operators may not be adjacent. Therefore X*−2 and U/−5 are illegal expressions. Brackets are used to surmount this obstacle so that the above expressions should be rewritten as:

$$X*(-2) \quad \text{and} \quad U/(-5)$$

How to Write Simple Arithmetical Programs in BASIC

2. Brackets or parentheses can surround any expression. An expression in brackets is treated as a single variable or constant in so far as it cannot be next to another variable, constant or bracketed expression without an operator in between.

    860   LET F = 3(A+B)

is incorrect and should be rewritten as

    860   LET F = 3*(A+B)

Brackets can be nested to any depth within an arithmetic expression. Redundant brackets are ignored by the compiler so that if in doubt as to the order of evaluation of a complicated expression (which is described below) you should use brackets to clarify matters. They should however always occur in pairs. Where possible beginners should avoid involved sequences of nested brackets and use many simple assignment statements to obtain the desired result.

3. Any expression may be signed, so that

    X/Y + (X/Y)   and   (+X/Y)

are identical expressions.

Order of Evaluation of Arithmetic Expressions

You may wonder what a BASIC compiler would put in J as the result of the assignment statement:

    870   LET J = 5 + 6*7

In reading any program but the simplest you will inevitably encounter assignment statements with more than a single arithmetic operator. The rules governing the order of evaluation of such arithmetic expressions are given below.

1. When there are no brackets all exponentiations are done first, then multiplications and divisions, and lastly additions and subtractions. Therefore the value of J in the above statement would be equivalent to 5 + (6*7) = 47. In the following statement:

    880   LET V = 56 + 7*3↑4

The value of V would be equivalent to 56 + (7*81) = 623.

2. If there is more than one arithmetic operator of the same hierarchical value (i.e. + and −; * and /) operations are done in order from left to right.

3. When there are sets of nested brackets the innermost are evaluated first. This process continues in an outwards direction until the outermost pair are dealt with, e.g.

890   LET F = 2 + (3 * (2↑ (3 + 2) − (6*5)))

would be evaluated in the stages:

F = 2 + (3 * (2↑5 − 30))
F = 2 + (3 * 2)
F = 2 + 6 = 8.

Brackets can be used to alter the normal hierarchy of arithmetic operations. The following statement is evaluated in the order listed below it where the second subtraction is computed before the exponentiation and the first subtraction before the multiplication.

900   LET K = 2* (37 − 5↑(8 − 6))
K = 2* (37 − 5↑2)
K = 2* (37 − 25)
K = 2*12
K = 24

In the following statements A has the value 2, B the value 5 and C the value 3. After each expression the steps in evaluation are worked out so that you can follow the order of evaluation.

1.   910   LET X = A + B * C↑2
X = 2 + 5 * 9
X = 2 + 45
X = 47

2.   920   LET X = ((A + B) * C)↑2
X = (7*3)↑2
X = 21↑2
X = 441

3.   930   LET X = (A + B)* C↑2
X = 7*3↑2
X = 7*9
X = 63

How to Write Simple Arithmetical Programs in BASIC

4. 940 LET X = (A + (B*C))↑2
            X = (2 + 15)↑2
            X = 17↑2
            X = 289

5. 950 LET X = (A + B) * (C↑2)
            X = (2 + 5) * 9
            X = 7 * 9
            X = 63

6. 960 LET X = A + ((B*C)↑2)
            X = 2 + (15↑2)
            X = 2 + 225
            X = 227

Thus three operators can be combined in six different ways. Wherever possible you should try to keep your assignment statements simple and clear both for your own sake and for the sake of future users of your programs. Brackets used judiciously can eliminate possible ambiguities but complicated nesting sequences should be eschewed. When in doubt, use more than one simple assignment statement. Using this technique, example 6 above could be rewritten as:

      960   LET X = B*C
      970   LET X = X↑2
      980   LET X = A + X

Multiple Assignment Statement

Some versions of BASIC (listed in Chapter 12) allow the facility of storing in several variables a constant, variable or result of an arithmetic expression, using one statement, known as a multiple assignment statement.

      990   LET K = L = M = N = 1

An evaluated expression could be stored in several variables by a statement of the type:

      1000   LET X = N = J = H = P7 = V↑3 − 22472*A

If you are unsure as to whether you will always be using a program on a system which allows this facility, it is best avoided or you will have to make tiresome program amendments when you encounter a system which does not permit multiple assignment statements.

Exercises 6.1

1. Write the following program correctly (9 statements need correction):

    ```
    90     REM AN INCORRECT PROGRAM
    100    LET A = 7
    110    LET 5 = B
    120    LET C = 1,000
    130    LET E = (A↑3)
    140        D = 2.0
    150    LET E = − E
    160    LET D = D + 1
    170    LET F = 4 (C+D)
    180    LET G = A*(B+E(5−D)
    190    LET H = G*−E
    200    PRINT,
    210    LET K = H↑ + 2
    220    PRINT E, F  G, H
    99999  END
    ```

2. What values are stored in K,D,E and F at the end of the following sequence of statements?

    ```
    100    LET G = 10
    110    LET A = 2
    120    LET B = 480E−2 + 0.2
    130    LET K = (A + 2)↑(B/G)
    140    LET D = 8*B+G↑A−1
    150    LET E = 180/(B*(A↑(B−2) + 4))
    160    LET F = B↑2↑A + G*4/5
    ```

Please turn to the answers on page 140 to see if you have answered the above questions correctly and can understand the principles by which the correct answers were obtained. These principles are explained there. If you feel satisfied that you understand the general form of

How to Write Simple Arithmetical Programs in BASIC

arithmetic expressions and the order of their evaluation you can proceed to the following questions which are short programs. If you have ready access to a terminal you can type them into the computer and ascertain the numerical answers to them as well as finding out if your solution is feasible.

3. Assign values to A,B,C and X and print the value of $AX^2 + BX + C$.

4. Print on the first line the integers 1–4, compute and print on the second line their reciprocals, on the third line compute and print their squares and on the fourth line compute and print their cubes.

5. Assign values to P,Q and R and compute and print the value of X in the expression:

$$X = \frac{PQ + QR}{P^2 + Q^2} \div \frac{Q^2 - QR}{P^2 + PQ}$$

The next three questions should be answered without using the square-root function which you have not so far encountered in BASIC.

6. Compute and print the roots of the equation $5x^2 - 9x - 6 = 0$ using the formula:

$$x = \frac{-b \pm \sqrt{(b^2 - 4ac)}}{2a}$$

7. Compute and print the length of the hypotenuse of a right-angled triangle with smaller sides of lengths 65 cm and 72 cm.

8. Print the time of swing (t) of a simple pendulum of length (L) 200 cm from the formula $t = 2\pi\sqrt{(L/g)}$. Assume $\pi = 3.14$ and $g = 980.67$ cm/s^2.

Standard Functions

High-level computer languages usually contain expressions for the automatic calculation of frequently used functions such as square roots and logarithms. (You will have already encountered one method of calculating a square root in the exercises you have just done.) The provision of these functions for procedures which are frequently required saves time and effort as the programmer does not have the chore of inserting statements to calculate the appropriate series for a trigonometric function. Tables are not used by the computer for this type of function. The computer calculates from a series such functions as cosines and tangents. The general form of a function is:

FNAME(e)

where e, the argument of the function, is any valid arithmetic expression and FNAME a function name. The mathematical functions usually provided are:

SIN
COS } (The argument must be in radians *not* degrees.)
TAN

ATN   The arctangent (in radians) of the argument.
LOG   Natural logarithm (base e).
EXP   The value of e raised to the power of the argument.
SQR   The positive square root of the argument.
ABS   The absolute value of the argument.
SGN   The sign of the argument. Gives a value of −1 when the argument is negative, 0 when it is zero and +1 when it is positive.
INT   The greatest integer less than or equal to the argument.

A function can be used in any place, such as a PRINT statement, where an arithmetic expression is valid. Functions can be combined with themselves, variables and constants in arithmetic expressions. A function can be an argument of a function, e.g.

900   LET Y = SQR(ABS(X+7))

Functions are evaluated before any other operator in the arithmetic expressions where they are present. Some typical examples of the use of functions in statements could be:

910   LET A = LOG(X/Y) − COS(P*Q)
920   LET R = SQR(ABS(V↑2 − W↑2)) + 211268
930   PRINT D, LOG(D), E+F, SQR(E+F)

How to Write Simple Arithmetical Programs in BASIC

You must remember that the argument of the trigonometric functions must be in radians. A useful method of conversions from degrees to radians is to multiply by .0174533 or divide by 57.2957795. Thus to place the cosine of 25 degrees in J the correct statement could be:

940   LET J = COS(25* .0174533)

The LOG function works with natural logarithms. An error message will be printed if the argument is zero or negative. If you want to find a logarithm to base 10 you must divide the natural logarithm of the argument by the natural logarithm of 10. Therefore a statement to compute $\log_{10} 7$ could be:

950   LET K = LOG(7)/LOG(10)

The argument of the SQR function should be positive and greater than zero. The use of this function is generally quicker than the method by which you probably found the square root in the exercises earlier in this chapter and should be preferred.

The INT function may be given unexpected results with a negative number if you have not fully understood that it *never* gives a value greater than the argument. Therefore INT(−3.001) and INT(−3.999) both have the value −4.

If you want to round a constant to the nearest integer (so that 4.5 would be rounded to 5 and −4.5 to −4) the correct statement could be:

960   LET R = INT(N + .5)

Using the above statement you can verify that the following values of R would be computed from the values of N.

N	R
11.2	11
17.8	18
−11.2	−11
−17.8	−18
.7	1
.4	0
−.7	−1
−.4	0

If you need to round a value to the nearest tenth, a suitable statement could be:

970   LET R = INT(10*N + .5)/10

You can verify that, if N was 12.36, R would be 12.4, and if N was 17.69, R would be 17.7.

There is a further standard function in BASIC, RND, which will generate a random number. The use of this is discussed on page 97.

Simple Data Entry

Your programs so far have all dealt with numerical data put as constants into the program. This has made the programs rigid. If you had wanted to calculate log(x) for three different values of x it would have been necessary to have three statements of the form:

980   LET X = (desired value)

This technique would obviously become cumbrous for realistic programs where you wanted to evaluate an expression for many different values of variables.

The READ and DATA statements are used together (so that one can never appear in a program without the other) and will enable many variable values to be entered in a simpler manner than using many assignment statements. The following sections of program show how the values 1—5 can be put in variables A—E by assignment statements and then more elegantly and economically by the use of READ and DATA.

1. *Using Assignment statements*

    990   LET A = 1
    1000 LET B = 2
    1010 LET C = 3
    1020 LET D = 4
    1030 LET E = 5

2. *Using READ and DATA statements*

    1040 DATA 1,2,3,4,5
    1050 READ A,B,C,D,E

You can visualise that a DATA statement puts a list of constants in the computer store and that DATA statements put data in this list in

How to Write Simple Arithmetical Programs in BASIC 65

the order in which they appear in a program. Therefore all the DATA statements in a program can be considered to form a continuous list of values. These statements need not necessarily precede a READ statement and can occur at any place in a program before the END statement. The above example 2 could have been rewritten as:

```
1060   DATA 1,2,3
1070   READ A,B,C,D,E
1080   DATA 4
1090   REM LAST DATA STATEMENT
1100   DATA 5
```

It should be remembered that items in a DATA statement are separated by commas.

The READ statement puts the next items in the data list into the variables following the command READ. One can imagine a pointer which at the start of the program is set at the head of the data list and advances one place each time a value is processed by a READ statement. At the end of the following sequence of instructions:

```
1110   DATA 1,4,76,69
1120   READ Q
1130   DATA 45,-3,16
1140   READ R,T,U,V
1150   READ A,B,C,D
1160   DATA -17,5
```

the values of the variables would be:

$Q = 1$
$R = 4$
$T = 76$
$U = 69$
$V = 45$
$A = -3$
$B = 16$
$C = -17$
$D = 5$

If a program tries to read more data than is present on the data list a message will be typed out at the terminal.

The use of the READ and DATA statements can enable the same program to be run many times with different data in a simpler way than would be possible by altering all the assignment statements. If the above technique is used to place numeric values in variables, only the DATA statements need to be altered, and if many values are inserted in a single statement the alteration of a program to allow the processing of different values is reduced to a minimum. Often the alteration of a single DATA line will suffice.

It is sometimes desired to process the same data more than once in a single program: the RESTORE command then sets the imaginary pointer to the very beginning of the data list so that the next READ statement after the RESTORE will deal with the first item on the data list. The form of the command is:

    1170   RESTORE

At the end of the following sequence of statements:

    1180   DATA −28.10,19.4
    1190   READ V,W
    1200   RESTORE
    1210   READ E,F

the values of the variables would be:

    $V = 28.1$
    $W = 19.4$
    $E = 28.1$
    $F = 19.4$

Data Entry during Program Execution

You may sometimes wish to enter data during the actual running of the program, especially after seeing previous results. It is faster and more economical to enter data by DATA and READ statements but the use of the INPUT statement for direct data entry enables true interaction to take place between user and computer. The general form of the statement is:

    INPUT (list of variable names)

After execution of the statement:

    1220   INPUT D,X

the computer would cease execution of the program until two numeric values had been typed. One would be stored in D and the other in X. Usually a question mark is typed and the user is expected to separate by commas the values he inserts.

Printing of Text

You will often want to print some explanation to add clarity to your results. Any set of symbols enclosed between quotation marks can be printed by a PRINT statement so that the statement:

    1230   "27 APRIL 1972"

would print:

27 APRIL 1972

on a line of output.

Spaces inside the quotation marks are copied literally on the output line as the above example demonstrates.

It is possible to print variable values and text on the same line with the same print statement. Variables and text can be presented inside the PRINT statement in any order. They are separated from one another by commas.

The following sequence of statements:

    1240   LET M = 4
    1250   LET E = 2
    1260   LET S = 3
    1270   PRINT "PRODUCT = ", M*E*S

would print:

PRODUCT =   24

If the items in a print list are separated by commas, each item is printed in a separate zone or field which in many versions of BASIC consists of 15 characters. It will be noticed that the quotation marks are *not* printed. The division of the print line on the terminal typewriter into zones facilitates the printing of results under headings, so that the following sequence of statements would align results under the appropriate heading.

    1280   LET M = 7
    1290   PRINT "M", "M SQUARED", "M CUBED"
    1300   PRINT M, M↑2, M↑3

M	M SQUARED	M CUBED
7	49	343

If a message is longer than a zone the printing automatically continues to the next zone without any space being left. It is helpful to use a message printing statement just before the INPUT statement described in the previous section of this chapter. This will remind the terminal operator of the variable names in which values are to be typed. A typical sequence of statements could be:

```
1310   PRINT "M", "E"
1320   INPUT M,E
```

which would produce on the terminal typewriter:

M	E
?	(typed after encountering INPUT).

It is even more useful to print a message for the terminal operator which will indicate some detail about the values which should be typed in, such as:

```
1330   PRINT "VOL.2DEC.", "FREQ.3 DIGITS"
```

which would produce output on the typewriter as:

VOL.2DEC.	FREQ.3DIGITS

The facility of printing messages before an INPUT statement can be used in various ways to indicate to the terminal operator the form of the values which are to be inserted.

Exercises 6.2

1. Input a number and print the number, its square, its cube, its square root and its reciprocal under appropriate printed headings.

2. Write short programs to input the appropriate values and print the result of the computations for:

    a. $a = 2pr \sin(\pi/p)$ (assume $\pi = 3.14$)
    b. $a = 2\sqrt{[b^2 + (4c^2/3)]}$

c. $a = -\dfrac{\cos^{(p+1)} y}{p+1}$

d. $a = \dfrac{1}{2} \log \left(\dfrac{1 + \sin x}{1 - \sin x} \right)$

e. $a = \left(\dfrac{2}{\pi x} \right)^{1/2} \sin x$

f. $a = \dfrac{ehp}{(\sin b)(h^4/16 + h^2 p^2)}$

g. $a = xs/2 - b^2/2 \log |x+s|$

h. $a = X - \left[\dfrac{b}{c(d - e^{f+q})} \right] \div \left[h_i^{j-k} + q^{m/(n+p)} \right]$

i. $a = e/\sqrt{[r^2 + (2\pi fl - 1/2\pi fc)^2]}$

3. Input the angles A, B, and C of a spherical triangle and compute the three "sides" a, b and c from the formula:

$$\tan(1/2a) = \dfrac{\sin(1/2E) \sin(A - 1/2E)}{\sin(B - 1/2E) \sin(C - 1/2E)}$$

and similar formulae for $\tan(1/2b)$ and $\tan(1/2c)$, where $E = A + B + C - \pi$ (radians).
(A, B and C are input in degrees; assume $\pi = 3.141593$).

Chapter 7

CONTROL STATEMENTS IN THE BASIC LANGUAGE

So far you are only able to express in the BASIC language the simplest type of flowchart which does not contain any decision boxes (which you will remember were represented by a diamond shaped drawing on the flowchart). The programs which you have been writing so far in BASIC have been purely linear, which imposes considerable limitations on the problems which you can solve at the computer terminal. At the moment you would have to assume that if you were solving a quadratic equation at the terminal the roots would be real as you have been given no instruction for testing whether $b^2 > 4ac$.

You cannot at the moment deal with programs where you are required to repeat the same instructions — the "loop" which was described in flowcharting terms in Chapter 4.

The GO TO Statement

This statement will interrupt the normal flow of the program. The next statement to be executed after a GO TO is the statement on the line number written after the words GO TO. The form of the statement is:

> GO TO line number

The statement GO TO 47 would obey the statement in line 47 of the program.

Control can be transferred by a GO TO statement forwards or backwards within a program so that the line number referred to in the GO TO statement can be greater or less than the line number of the GO TO statement itself.

The following example shows a possible use of the GO TO statement:

Control Statements in the BASIC Language

```
090    PRINT "TYPE AN INTEGER"
100    INPUT X
110    PRINT X, X*X
120    GO TO 90
```

This section of program would return for more input to be typed in as long as it was desired to print further values of numbers and their squares. It is a relatively crude method since there is no way out of the closed loop of statements, 90, 100, 110, 120. The program would be abandoned when it was considered that enough numbers had been entered. More realistic and sophisticated methods of solving the problem posed in the above sequence of instructions will be discussed in the next section of this chapter which describes the conditional statement.

Care should be taken to ensure that a GO TO statement always refers to an executable statement and not to a directive such as REM and DATA even though many versions of BASIC would automatically transfer control to the next executable statement.

The GO TO statement is sometimes useful for inserting extra statements in a program where there are not line numbers available to type in statements in their proper place, but this technique should be avoided by leaving gaps between the line numbers. In the following sequence of instructions it will be noticed that the READ statement has been omitted and the lines have been (foolishly) numbered so that the statement cannot be inserted before the PRINT statement.

```
121    DATA 17,72,5
122    PRINT A,B,C
(123-150 rest of program)
```

A GO TO statement can be used to ensure that the READ instruction is obeyed in its correct sequence in the following manner:

```
121    DATA 17,72,5
122    GO TO 160
(123-150 rest of original program — except for END statement)
160    READ A,B,C
170    PRINT A,B,C
180    GO TO 123
190    REM PROGRAM NOW RETURNS TO SEQUENCE
```

This technique is known as "patching" and the sequence of instructions 160-190 known as a "patch". If the scheme of line numbering recommended had been followed in the original sequence of instructions the missing READ statement could have been inserted by giving it one of the vacant line numbers between the DATA and PRINT statements (usually one of nine numbers). If the DATA statement had been numbered 120 and the PRINT statement 130 the missing statement could have been given any number in the range 121–129. Patching is at best a clumsy contrivance and emphasises the reasons for leaving gaps between statements when a program is originally written. Perhaps your only use of this technique will be for statement insertion in programs you inherit from elsewhere! Care must be taken if using a patch to make sure that the instruction replaced by the GO TO statement on the original program (the PRINT statement in the above example) is included in the patch. Any patch must have its line numbers less than the END statement — a reason for giving the END statement the largest statement number allowed by the compiler.

Comparisons in BASIC

Few serious and practical problems can be flowcharted for a computer in a linear manner; such a flow chart will almost certainly contain the diamond shaped boxes and make use of some of the looping or iterative techniques described in Chapter 4. You will remember that the diamond shaped box in the flowchart contained a relation such as A=B, $X \geqslant Y$, $D < G$.

The relational operators which are used for comparing values in BASIC are:

$$
\begin{aligned}
&= \quad \text{is equal to} \\
&<> \text{ is not equal to} \\
&> \quad \text{is greater than} \\
&>= \text{ is greater than or equal to} \\
&< \quad \text{is less than} \\
&<= \text{ is less than or equal to}
\end{aligned}
$$

These are the only relationships which can be expressed in most versions of BASIC. It will be noticed that three of the operators consist of two symbols and differ from the conventional mathematical notation owing to the limitations of the typewriter terminal keyboard. The correct order of symbols must always be used here so that $=>$ must not be used in place of $>=$.

Control Statements in the BASIC Language

The general form of a comparison in the BASIC language is:

$$\left.\begin{array}{c}\text{variable}\\ \text{expression}\end{array}\right\} \quad \begin{array}{c}\text{relational}\\ \text{operator}\end{array} \quad \left\{\begin{array}{c}\text{numeric constant}\\ \text{variable}\\ \text{expression}\end{array}\right.$$

Some valid comparisons would be:

$$X = 13$$
$$M <> E*S$$
$$Q > N$$
$$A\uparrow 4 >= 1296$$
$$P/(Y-I) < V*(J - 4)$$
$$SQR(T-V) <= H+L$$

Within an expression in a comparison the usual order of evaluation described in the previous chapter is followed. The = operator means exact equality unlike the use of this symbol in a LET statement. Care should be taken in comparing evaluated quantities for equality as two expressions which are thought to be equal may differ by a minute quantity owing to floating point representation of non-integer quantities. It is advisable to use the = operator only in comparing quantities which are absolutely certain to be integers. Thus instead of writing:

$$T + U = V/R$$

when it is uncertain that the expressions will be evaluated to exact integer values you should write:

$$ABS((T + U) - (V/R)) < 10E-6$$

Any small quantity which is capable of representation on the computer used and which can be ascertained from the appropriate manufacturer's programming manual may be substituted for $10E-6$.

The BASIC Conditional Statement

The form of the statement is:

    IF comparison THEN line number

e.g.
    IF $B\uparrow 2 > 4*A*C$ THEN 45
    IF M = 17 THEN 106

If the comparison is true the program obeys the statement in the line number after THEN. If it is not true, the next statement after the IF statement is obeyed. In the following sequence of statements:

```
200   LET I = 8
210   LET J = 5
220   IF I < J THEN 250
230   PRINT "FALSE"
240   GO TO 260
250   PRINT "TRUE"
260   (rest of program)
```

"FALSE" will be printed and the statement on line 250 will not be obeyed after THEN since the comparison I < J is not true.

Only the above form of statement may be used even though alternatives may sound reasonable and equivalent in English. Such would-be statements as:

```
IF Y = 13 THEN GO TO 165
```

should be avoided. A common mistake in writing the IF statement which is sometimes made by beginners is to put a comma before THEN which will in practice result in the compiler not being able to recognise the statement so that a diagnostic error will be printed during compilation.

The IF statement can be used for a realistic and more elegant solution of the problem encountered at the start of this chapter when it was desired to input numbers and print the numbers and their squares. If it was decided that four numbers would be read, the appropriate sequence of instructions would read:

```
270   LET K = 0
280   REM SETS COUNT TO ZERO
290   READ X
300   PRINT X,X*X
310   LET K = K + 1
320   REM AUGMENTS COUNT BY ONE
330   IF K < 4 THEN 290
340   (rest of program)
```

It will be seen from this example that a THEN can refer to line numbers less than its own statement number as well as those greater so that control can be transferred forwards or backwards within a program. In the above example you could rewrite the IF statement as:

Control Statements in the BASIC Language

```
330    IF K <> 4 THEN 290
```

but the double use of GO TO in the following version of the end of the above sequence of statements should be avoided.

```
330    IF K = 4 THEN GO TO 350
340    GO TO 290
350    (rest of program)
```

To a beginner it may be more obvious to test the count for equality but the double jump would be obvious at the flowcharting stage of the program. Such a technique is perfectly correct, but clumsy, and requires an extra GO TO statement.

Sometimes you may wish to have alternative endings for your program. The statement STOP can be used at any point in the program where you wish to bring the computation to a halt. This is an alternative to writing GO TO line number of END statement but does not replace the need for having an END statement to conclude the text of each program. There can be any number of STOP statements in a program.

The following small program shows the use of the STOP statement in a branching program. Two numbers are input and their relationship is printed.

```
360      INPUT G,H
370      IF G > H THEN 410
380      IF G = H THEN 430
390      PRINT "LESS"
400      STOP
410      PRINT "GREATER"
420      STOP
430      PRINT "EQUAL"
99999    END
```

The STOP statements replace GO TO 99999.

There are four important uses to a statement to a programmer. These are:

1. Counting a number of items for identical processing.
2. Terminating processing by reading a predetermined character terminating a number of items.
3. Taking alternative action as a result of a computed value.

4. Stopping an iteration when the difference between two iterations is so small as to be insignificant.

1. Counts

The use of the IF statement in processing a predetermined number of items has already been discussed in connection with the program on page 740. That example set the count to the initial value of zero. It is possible (and more logical to some programmers) to set the count initially to 1. If this had been done the program would have read:

```
440   LET K = 1
450   REM SETS COUNT TO ONE
460   READ X
470   PRINT X,X*X
480   LET K = K + 1
490   REM AUGMENTS COUNT BY ONE
500   IF K < 5 THEN 460
```

There are numerous alternatives of using a count for the above program, such as:

```
510   LET K = 1
520   READ X
530   PRINT X,X*X
540   REM TEST PRECEDES AUGMENTATION OF COUNT
550   IF K = 4 THEN 580
560   LET K = K + 1
570   GO TO 520
580   (rest of program)
```

Probably the first method of solving this problem is the clearest.

2. Termination of Processing by Reading of a Predetermined Character

Often you will not want to arbitrarily fix the number of input items but would prefer to deal with a variable number of items each time a program is used. In that case you must type a "sentinel" when you have finished entering the valid items for processing. This sentinel must be

Control Statements in the BASIC Language

some value that would not normally occur in the data. The following sequence of statements expresses the INPUT program in a form where printing of values would be terminated when −1 is typed.

```
590    PRINT "TYPE −1 WHEN YOU WISH TO FINISH"
600    INPUT X
610    IF X = −1 THEN 99999
620    PRINT X,X*X
630    GO TO 600
99999  END
```

Care should be taken to ensure that the sentinel is not a value which would ever occur as valid data. You should also ensure by care in flow-charting that the sentinel is never processed in the same manner as the valid input. This would occur if statements 610 and 620 were interchanged in the above example.

Although the sentinel technique is usually used to mark the end of processing it can be used similarly to mark the end of one loop and the commencement of another section of program. The following program prints input integers and their mean in series which are terminated by −1. An entry of zero terminates the whole program.

```
640    REM MESSAGE TO OPERATOR
650    PRINT "TYPE −1 AT END OF SERIES, 0 AT END
                                OF ALL SERIES"
660    LET K = 0
670    LET N = 0
680    REM SETS COUNT AND TOTAL TO ZERO
690    INPUT X
700    LET K = K + 1
710    REM AUGMENTS COUNT
720    IF X < 1 THEN 770
730    PRINT X
740    LET N = N + X
750    REM AUGMENTS TOTAL
760    GO TO 690
770    PRINT "AVERAGE = ", N/(K−1)
780    REM TEST FOR END OF ALL SERIES
790    IF X = −1 THEN 660
99999  END
```

(What alteration would you make to statement 720 if valid items were not confined to integers?)

It can be seen from the above example that a variety of different sentinels can be used for different purposes in a program. When using the sentinel technique it is always advisable to type a message defining the sentinel value(s) for the operator.

3. Taking Alternative Action as a Result of a Computed Value

The taking of action as a result of a count augmented during the execution of the program, which was described in section 1 of this chapter, is a special case of the above technique. The following sequence of statements inputs values for a, b and c as coefficients of the general quadratic:

$$ax^2 + bx + c = 0$$

and branches if $b^2 \leqslant 4ac$.

```
800   INPUT A,B,C
810   LET D = B*B − 4*A*C
820   IF D<=0 THEN 900
830   (rest of program)
```

You will see that the formula $b^2 - 4ac$ is evaluated before the test since it will be needed in the path of the program which evaluates the values of x. If statement 810 read:

```
810   IF B*B <= 4*A*C THEN 900
```

b^2 and $4ac$ would have to be recalculated if the equation had real roots (which is assumed to be the most likely branch of the program).

4. Termination of Iterative Loops

Iteration techniques are of great importance in numerical analysis. The use of such a technique to find a square root was described with a flow-chart in Chapter 4. The loop in the flowchart was terminated when the difference between successive iterations was less than 10^{-6}. The following sequence of instructions is a translation of the flowchart into BASIC.

Control Statements in the BASIC Language

```
  840   INPUT N
  850   IF N <=0 THEN 950
  860   REM TEST FOR ZERO OR NEGATIVE INPUT
  870   LET X = 1
  880   REM START OF LOOP
  890   LET S = (X+N/X)/2
  900   IF ABS(X–S) < 1E–6 THEN 930
  910   LET X = S
  920   GO TO 890
  930   PRINT "SQUARE ROOT OF", N, "=", S
  940   STOP
  950   PRINT "ERROR, N = ", N
99999   END
```

Whenever an IF statement is used care should be taken to ensure that the appropriate sequence of statements follows the appropriate branch — confusion here can be perplexing to a beginner. When flowcharting a problem a solution should be worked by hand with small samples of data to ensure that branches of an IF statement contain the correct instructions.

You will have noticed that the algebraic comparisons ≯ and ≮ are not found in BASIC. <= can be used for ≯ and > = for ≮.

Care should be taken to guard against infinite loops when one branch of an IF statement reverts to a section of program before the IF statement. Sometimes in a program of statements like:

```
  960   IF D > E THEN 840
```

there is a faint possibility that D may always be computed less than E so that the program obeys the same loop indefinitely. If this happens inadvertently when you are at a terminal you will notice that the program seems to be taking longer to execute than expected. In such an event the program should be halted from the keyboard and re-run with the insertion of PRINT statements for the compared values if examination of the problem away from the terminal does not indicate the fault. Unfamiliarity with iterative techniques may lead to values being used which will diverge instead of producing the desired convergence.

Many versions of BASIC have considerable variety of IF statements which transcend some of the limitations of the common version described in this chapter. For instance, the Honeywell Time Sharing BASIC User's Guide contains a three-branch IF statement of the form:

IF expression, lineno, lineno, lineno

Control is transferred to the first line number if the value of the expression is negative, the second if it is zero and the third if it is positive.

The BASIC-PLUS supplied for the PDP 11 computer, and the Computer Technology Ltd BASIC for Modular One computers allow simple comparisons to be linked by the operators AND and OR, so that such statements as:

970   IF (D=9 OR D < 67) AND (T = 6 AND V > 4)
                                                    THEN 840

are possible and save a multiplicity of simple IF statements.

Such refinements of the IF statement as are found in various extensions to BASIC should however only be used if you are certain to be always running a program on a certain type of computer and do not wish to make the program available for types of computer which have not implemented such refinements as are not common to all versions of the BASIC language.

The Computed GO TO Statement

This additional control statement is found in many versions of BASIC and is more likely to be included in the particular dialect of BASIC you are using than the extensions to the IF statement described above. Nevertheless, you should be cautious about using this facility if you are likely to transfer your program to a computer system for which this statement is not implemented. The usual form of this statement is:

ON variable-name or arithmetic expression GO TO list of line numbers

although there is a variant:

GO TO list of line numbers ON variable-name or arithmetic expression

In the statement:

980   ON M GO TO 140, 350, 110, 2090

control would be transferred to line 140 if M had the value of 1, to 350 if 2, to 110 if 3, and if M had the value of 4 control would go to line 2090.

Control Statements in the BASIC Language

The following program reads a number and prints whether it is odd or even and utilises the ON GO TO technique.

```
  990  REM MESSAGE FOR OPERATOR
 1000  PRINT "INPUT AN INTEGER"
 1010  READ Z
 1020  LET A = Z-2*INT(Z/2) +1
 1030  REM A = 1 FOR EVEN, 2 FOR ODD
 1040  ON A GO TO 1050, 1070
 1050  PRINT "EVEN"
 1060  STOP
 1070  PRINT "ODD"
99999  END
```

Care should be taken to ensure that the value of the expression following ON is not zero (hence the addition of one to the remainder in the above example), negative, or an integer greater than the number of line numbers in the list following GO TO. If this happens execution of the program will be halted and an error message typed out.

An arithmetic expression can be substituted for the variable after ON so that in the above example the addition of 1 could be omitted in line 1020 and line 1040 could read:

```
 1040  ON A + 1 GO TO 1050, 1070
```

When an expression is evaluated after ON it is truncated to the nearest integer.

The power of a computed GO TO statement increases with the number of alternatives. If there are many paths which a program may follow, the use of a computed GO TO statement saves many simple IF statements where only two branches are possible.

The following program reads an integer and prints in words the remainder when divided by 7.

```
 1080  REM MESSAGE FOR OPERATOR
 1090  PRINT "TYPE A POSITIVE INTEGER"
 1100  INPUT A
 1110  ON A -7*INT(A/7) +1 GO TO 1120, 1140, 1160,
                           1180, 1200, 1220, 1240
 1120  PRINT "ZERO"
 1130  STOP
 1140  PRINT "ONE"
```

```
1150  STOP
1160  PRINT "TWO"
1170  STOP
1180  PRINT "THREE"
1190  STOP
1200  PRINT "FOUR"
1210  STOP
1220  PRINT "FIVE"
1230  STOP
1240  PRINT "SIX"
99999 END
```

Exercises 7.1

1. Print the integers 1–100 with their squares, cubes, square roots and cube roots.

2. Compute and print the reciprocals of the integers 2–100.

3. Input 10 numbers and calculate their mean.

4. Input 10 pairs of numbers representing the smaller sides of 10 right-angled triangles and print the 10 hypotenuse values.

5. Print a table of circles with areas increasing in steps of 1 m^2 from 1 m^2 to 100 m^2 and their corresponding radii. (Assuming $\pi = 3.14$.)

6. $\pi/4 = 1 - 1/3 + 1/5 - 1/7 + 1/9 - \ldots$
   Evaluate 1000 terms of this series and print the value of π every 100 terms.

7. Compute and print the terms of the Fibonacci series:
   $$(x_{n+1} = x_n + x_{n-1})$$
   between 10^3 and 10^6. The initial terms are 0 1 1 2 3 5 8 . . . .

8. The solution of the simultaneous equations:
   $$ax + by + c = 0$$
   $$px + qy + r = 0$$

is given by
$$x = (br - cq)/(aq - bq)$$
$$y = (pc - ar)/(aq - bq)$$

Input a,b,c,p,q,r and compute and print x and y.
Print INDETERMINATE if $aq-bq = 0$.
Print NOT INDEPENDENT if $a/p = b/q = c/r$.

Chapter 8

LOOPS AND SUBSCRIPTED VARIABLES

All loops can be programmed by means of the IF statement which was described in the previous chapter. The use of the FOR and NEXT statement discussed below does however provide a more elegant and economic method of programming loops. This statement is designed especially for looping and keeping counters, in contrast to the IF statement which as you have discovered has many other uses (such as testing for input errors) besides controlling loops. The FOR statement gives control of looping with fewer instructions than the use of IF, whilst the testing of the count is automatic. This statement also makes programs more readable and comprehensible.

A typical FOR statement would be:

    100   FOR N = A TO M STEP Q

N is often known as the *controlled variable*. It is first given the value of A (initial value), then the loop is repeated with successive increments of Q (increment), until the loop is obeyed the last time with A having the value of M (terminal value). The loop consists of all statements between FOR and a NEXT statement which has the form:

    NEXT controlled variable.

In the statements:

    110   FOR H = 10 TO 14 STEP 2
    120   LET A = H–3
    130   LET R = A*A
    140   PRINT R
    150   NEXT H

Loops and Subscripted Variables 85

The program would print:

49
81
121

The form of the FOR statement is:

FOR controlled variable = initial value TO terminal value
STEP increment

The initial and terminal values and the increment can be variables, constants or arithmetic expressions. If the increment is 1 the STEP section of the statement can be omitted, as in the example below which uses a FOR statement for the program printing four input values and their squares, which was written with an IF statement in the previous chapter.

```
160   FOR K = 1 TO 4
170   PRINT "TYPE AN INTEGER"
180   REM MESSAGE FOR OPERATOR
190   INPUT X
200   PRINT X,X*X
210   NEXT K
```

This sequence of instructions, if compared with the corresponding sequence in the previous chapter, shows the economy of the use of the FOR statement to control loops.

Some examples of legal FOR statements in BASIC are:

```
FOR N = M↑3 − P TO ABS(I + J)
FOR T = A to 8.5 STEP .5
FOR L = 10 TO 1 STEP −1
FOR Y = −B TO −(U*D) STEP −5
```

A FOR statement must never appear without a corresponding NEXT. Your program will not compile and a diagnostic message will be printed if the relevant NEXT statement is omitted.

Subscripted variables (which will be defined in a later part of this chapter) may not be used as the controlled variable of a FOR statement.

The third example of a FOR statement listed above shows the use of a negative increment. Care should be taken here to ensure that the terminal value is less than the initial value or the program may continue indefinitely in the FOR loop. This occasion could arise when expressions are used for the initial value, terminal value or increment.

If successive additions of the increment to the initial value do not exactly produce the terminal value, the loop is executed for the last time (if the increment is positive) when the controlled variable has the greatest value not more than the terminal value. In the following example:

FOR G = 2 TO 13 STEP 3

the loops would be executed with G taking successive values of 2,5,8,11. In the case of a negative increment in a loop where the terminal value would not be exactly reached, the loop would be executed for the last time with the controlled variable having the least value not less than the terminal value. In the following example:

FOR Q = −5 TO −11 STEP −4

the loop would be executed with G taking successive values of −5 and −9. Care should be taken in loops which contain quantities which are not exact integers. In the statement:

FOR L = 1 TO 1.009 STEP .001

there is a possibility that owing to the representation of floating point numbers the continued addition of .001 may result in a value slightly in excess of 1.009 so that the last iteration would not be performed. The statement is better written as:

FOR L = 1 TO 1.0091 STEP .001

which ensures that the last iteration is performed.

On exit from a loop the controlled variable usually retains the value it possessed the last time the loop was executed but there are some variations here and the programming manual of the system used should be consulted on this point.

The loop between FOR and NEXT can be executed:

1. Never. In some versions of BASIC (e.g. the version used by IBM System 3) a loop is skipped over if the initial value is greater than the terminal value and the increment is positive — thus obviating the execution of an infinite loop as mentioned above.
2. An infinite number of times. This can occur when the value of the increment is zero — unless there is a jump out of the loop by an IF or GO TO statement.

Loops and Subscripted Variables

3. Once. This can occur when the terminal and initial values are identical, as from unforeseen data insertions. This would occur in the following sequence of statements if 3 were typed in at the INPUT halt.

```
220   LET R = 7
230   LET T = R + 2
240   PRINT "INPUT AN INTEGER"
250   INPUT Y
260   LET P = SQR(T)
270   FOR U = P TO Y STEP 2
280   PRINT U,U*U,U↑3, U↑4
290   NEXT U
```

Usually the initial value (if a variable) can be modified during the execution of a loop and (if an expression) variables within that value can be modified although some clarity is then lost. Any variable in the terminal value or increment should definitely *not* be altered and although it is possible to alter the controlled variable (as in the following example):

```
300   FOR V = 3 TO 7
310   PRINT V,V*V
320   LET V = V + 4
330   NEXT V
```

(where the loop would only be executed once) such techniques are best avoided.

An IF or GO TO statement may be used to jump out of a loop (and not return) during execution, to omit statements within a loop and to jump out of (and later return) to a loop. An example of the last could be:

```
340   FOR W = 5 TO 9
350   LET X = W/2
360   IF X < = 3 THEN 400
370   LET Y = SQR(X)
380   PRINT Y
390   NEXT W
400   LET X = X + 1
410   GO TO 380
```

although it would be less clumsy to include statements 400 and 410 within the loop.

You must *never* however enter a loop after the FOR statement from outside the loop unless you have previously left the loop. In an example such as:

```
420   READ A,B,C
430   LET D = A + B
440   GO TO 470
450   LET E = A − B
460   FOR J = 1 TO 6
470   LET F = D*E/J
480   PRINT SQR(F)
490   NEXT J
```

the initialisation of the value of J is carelessly bypassed.

Loops can be nested within loops. The following program finds the means of five series of 10 numbers:

```
  500   REM START OF OUTER LOOP
  510   FOR K = 1 TO 5
  520   LET S = 0
  530   REM SETS TOTAL TO ZERO
  540   REM START OF INNER LOOP
  550   FOR L = 1 TO 10
  560   PRINT "TYPE A NUMBER"
  570   INPUT N
  580   LET S = S + N
  590   NEXT L
  600   LET M = S/10
  610   PRINT "SERIES", K, "MEAN = ", M
  620   NEXT K
99999   END
```

You must always ensure that the FOR and NEXT of inner loops are contained by the FOR and NEXT of the appropriate outer loop. To avoid confusion inner loops may be indented and lines drawn connecting them. *Figure 8.1* shows some examples of correct and incorrect use of the nesting technique. The lines cross one another in the incorrect examples.

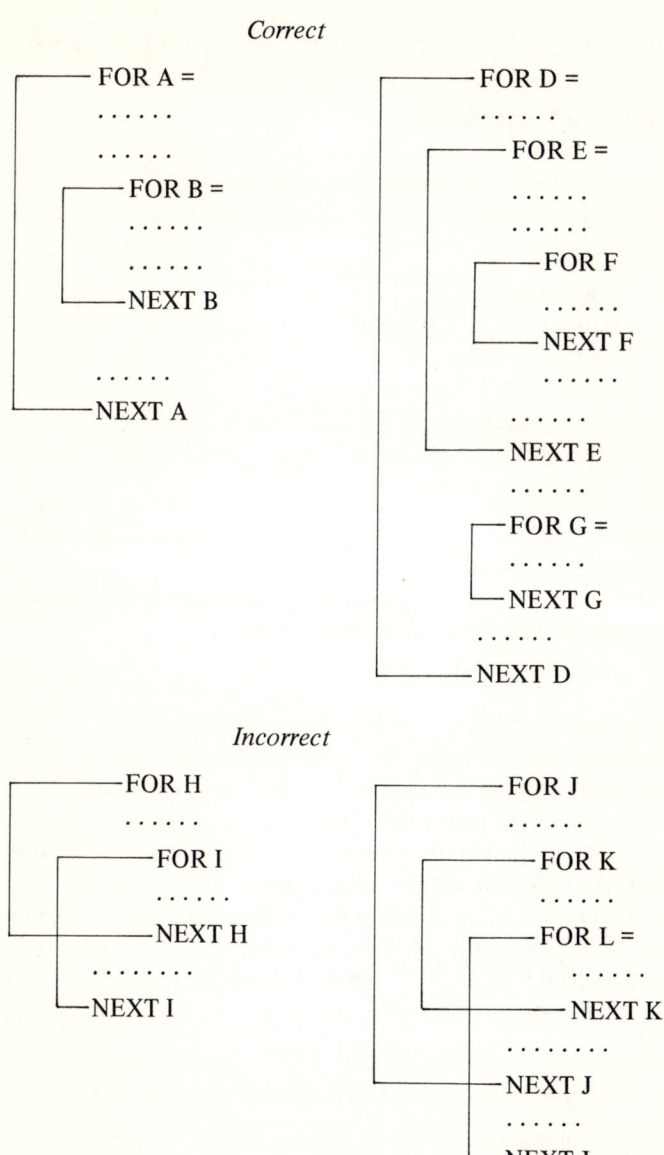

Figure 8.1 Examples of correct and incorrect use of the nesting technique

Exercises 8.1

Write programs for examples 1–6 of 7.1 using FOR statements.

Subscripted Variables

At the moment you cannot use looping techniques to read three numbers, store them and print their average. In the sequence of statements:

```
630   LET S = 0
640   FOR L = 1 TO 3
650   INPUT N
660   LET S = S + N
670   NEXT L
680   PRINT "MEAN = ", S/3
```

the values of the individual numbers typed in are lost so that this sequence would be no use if it was required to calculate deviations from the mean.

If you wanted to store the numbers as they were input you would have to have an input statement of the type:

```
650   INPUT X,Y,Z
```

and you would not be able to use a FOR statement.

The use of subscripted variables can enable problems like these to be done using looping techniques. You may be familiar with subscripted variables or arrays in mathematics where singly subscripted algebraic variables such as x_1, y_{11} are used for lists of items and doubly subscripted variables such as $e_{1,1}$ and $g_{4,6}$ are used for tables or matrices. If you wish to use an array with a subscript greater than 10 in a program the size of the array must be declared before the array is used in the program. A DIM statement is used for this purpose. It reserves space in the computer store for the tables you need. The form of the DIM statement is:

DIM variable name (range), variable name (range) . . . .

For a list or one-dimensional array the range is the upper bound of the array, so that the statement:

```
690   DIM A(25), L(153)
```

Loops and Subscripted Variables

would reserve store for an array A with upper bound 25 and an array L with upper bound 153.

For a two-dimensional array or matrix two integers are needed to define the range. The first integer is the upper bound of the rows, the second is the upper bound of the columns. The statement:

    700   DIM E(4,5), Y(7,15)

would reserve space for a matrix E with 4 rows and 5 columns and a matrix Y with 7 rows and 15 columns.

The variable name used for an array has no connection with the same variable name used as a simple variable, so that in the sequence of statements:

    710   DIM V(20)
    720   LET V = 9
    725   LET V6 = V+2

statements 720 and 725 would in no way affect any item in the array V. All letters of the alphabet can be used once (and only once) in a DIM statement so that no more than 26 arrays can be used in a single program. A letter cannot be used for both a one- and two-dimensional array in the same program. To avoid confusion it is better (except where all available letters are used) not to use the same letter to denote simple unsubscripted variables and arrays.

If a one-dimensional array variable is mentioned in a program without a preceding DIM statement it is assumed that the upper bound of the array is 10. If a two-dimensional item is mentioned store is reserved for a 10 by 10 matrix. Thus, in respect of matrices, a great deal of store can be saved by the use of the DIM statement.

You will have to consult your own manufacturer's programming manual as to whether the items of an array start at 0 or 1. This is also mentioned in Chapter 12 which treats of some of the differences found in the versions of BASIC you are likely to encounter. If a one-dimensional array item is used without a DIM statement, versions of BASIC which start arrays at 0 will save space for 11 elements.

You will have to make an estimate of the size of the array if you need to use a DIM statement, so that you can fix the upper bound. Unlike some computer languages, BASIC does not possess the facility of fixing the upper bound by a variable, so that a would-be statement of the type:

    730   DIM B(25), M(I)

is illegal. If you wish to use an array of varying size in different runs of a program you must insert in the DIM statement the maximum upper bound(s) which you think you will need to use. Your manufacturer's programming manual will tell you the maximum size allowed for arrays. Only integers are allowed to express the upper bound so that numbers in a DIM statement such as 5. and 100.0 would be illegal.

An item in an array is referred to by the variable name followed by an integer or arithmetic expression in brackets (or two integers or arithmetic expressions in the case of a matrix). These must *not* be confused with ordinary variables using an unbracketed number, such as E4, J9. Some examples of array elements are:

$$D(19), K(V), J(V+4), W(R*E), Y(2,3), M(R,T), X(U-1,V*Z)$$

It is better to evaluate more complicated expressions for the subscript (if indeed these are really necessary) in a LET statement. In most versions of BASIC a subscript expression is truncated to form an integer, so that in the following sequence of statements:

```
740   LET E = 7.5
750   LET F = (E + .5)/20
760   READ Y(E + F)
```

the subscript of Y which is 7.9 would be truncated to 7. Few versions of BASIC allow a subscript to be itself a subscripted variable, so that a reference of the type R(C(J)) should be avoided. Naturally a subscript should be less than the upper bound of the array. The problem defined at the start of this section (to input three numbers, print their mean, and store the numbers using a loop) can be solved using the following sequence of statements:

```
770   LET S = 0
780   FOR L = 1 TO 3
790   INPUT N(L)
800   LET S = S + N(L)
810   NEXT L
820   PRINT "MEAN = ", S/3
```

No DIM statement is needed in the above example since the array only contains three elements (unless you are of a parsimonious turn of mind and wish to save seven units of store!).

The following sequence of statements includes a DIM statement since

Loops and Subscripted Variables 93

it reads 20 numbers from a DATA list, prints their mean and then prints the numbers in the reverse order to that in which they were read.

```
830    DATA (20 numbers)
840    DIM E(20)
850    LET S = 0
860    FOR K = 1 TO 20
870    READ E(K)
880    LET S = S + E(K)
890    NEXT K
900    PRINT "MEAN = ", S/20
910    FOR N = 20 TO 1 STEP −1
920    PRINT E(N)
930    NEXT N
```

(The above example, as all examples in this book, assumes that arrays start at 1.)

For matrix manipulation the great majority of versions of BASIC include powerful matrix instructions which will, amongst other facilities, read and print matrices or tables with a single statement. These are described in Chapter 13.

The following example shows how elements of a matrix with 8 columns and 6 rows can be read using FOR statements:

```
940    DATA (24 numbers)
950    DATA (24 numbers)
960    DIM D(6,8)
970    REM M COUNTS ROWS, N COUNTS COLUMNS
980    FOR M = 1 TO 6
990    FOR N = 1 TO 8
1000   READ D(M,N)
1010   NEXT N
1020   NEXT M
```

The following example is a continuation of the above sequence. It uses both one- and two-dimensional arrays. It stores the sum of each row of the above matrix in G(1) to G(6).

```
1030   DIM G(6)
1040   REM CLEARS TOTALS
1050   FOR N = 1 TO 6
1060   LET G(N) = 0
```

```
1070   NEXT N
1080   REM M COUNTS ROWS, N COUNTS COLUMNS
1090   FOR M = 1 TO 6
1100   FOR N = 1 TO 8
1110   LET G(M) = G(M) + D(M,N)
1120   NEXT N
1130   NEXT M
```

Exercises 8.2

1. Read 10 numbers from a data list, print their mean and print the number with the greatest absolute deviation from the mean.

2. Write a program to divide each element of a matrix with 5 rows and 3 columns by the largest element.

3. Write a program to print out the largest element of a matrix with 3 rows and 4 columns and to print the row and column of the largest element.

4. Print the prime numbers between 3 and 100.

5. Print a square of 5 rows and 5 columns with each of the rows and columns containing once only each of the numbers 1–5 (Latin square).

6. Read from a data list a series of positive numbers ending with −1 and print the average, the largest and smallest of the numbers. Assume there are no more than 60 numbers.

7. Read numbers from a data list, the last number of which is 0, and print out the number of negative items you have read.

8. Read numbers from a data list into a 5 x 3 matrix and transpose the first and third rows of the matrix. Print out the matrix before and after this transposition with each row on a separate line.

Chapter 9

FUNCTIONS AND SUBROUTINES

You will have discovered the usefulness of the standard functions in many programs. Some versions of BASIC have functions additional to those given on page 62 and you may have felt that in some programs some additional function which you would define yourself would save programming effort.

Before you can use a function of your own you must define it. The appropriate BASIC statement is the DEF statement. This occupies a single line so that you must ensure that a function you wish to use can be expressed in a single line since continuation lines are not allowed. You cannot use a mnemonic name for a BASIC function as you could with some high-level computer languages. A name of a user-defined function consists of the letters FN followed by a character in the range A–Z so that in a single program you can only use 26 of your own functions. The form of the DEF statement is:

DEF function-name (dummy variable) = arithmetic expression

The dummy variable is a variable name consisting of a single unsubscripted letter of the alphabet and never contains an actual numerical value, so that if the function:

100   DEF FNG(T) = T↑2 + T↑3

was defined, *the variable T could be used at will in the program and would not affect in any way the function definition.*

The dummy variable is replaced by a variable or arithmetic expression in the actual program when the function is used. It is important to realise that no evaluation of the function takes place in the DEF statement — only when the function is called or invoked in the program. The following sequence of instructions show actual use of a user-defined function. The sequence reads three angles of a triangle in degrees from a data list and prints their sines. It will be noticed that the DEF statement makes use of the standard SIN function. The use of these standard functions is allowed in the functions you define yourself.

```
110   DEF FNS(A) = SIN(A*.017453)
120   FOR K = 1 TO 3
130   READ X(K)
140   REM USER FUNCTION CALLED NOW
150   LET R = FNS(X(K))
160   PRINT "SINE IS", R
170   NEXT K
```

The values of X(1), X(2) and X(3) are in turn substituted for the dummy variable A in the above section of program.

Other possible arguments for a function could be:

```
FNS(45)
FNS(A*(B-C))
FNS(ABS(V/Q))
```

A user-defined function can be used in many types of BASIC statements either in isolation or as part of an arithmetic expression, e.g.

```
IF N > FNA(D+2.5) THEN 450
FOR T = K TO FNQ(W/Z) STEP 5
PRINT "VALUE IS", FNG(A-P)
LET R = U + ABS (G = 4.5* (FND(E/F)))
```

Only rarely in some versions of BASIC can a user-defined function use itself in its call or (in computer science parlance) be used recursively. A function to evaluate fourth powers should not in the majority of versions of BASIC be written in the manner shown below:

```
180   DEF FNF(E) = E↑2
190   LET R = Y − FNF(FNF(T))
```

A user-defined function should not in its definition reference another function which calls on the function being defined. (This is mutual recursion − a compiler writer's nightmare!) Statements like the following should be avoided:

```
200   DEF FNT(Y) = V − J/(FNE(Y))
210   DEF FNE(X) = FNT(X) − C
```

Functions and Subroutines

A user-defined function need not contain the dummy variable in the arithmetic expression in its definition, e.g.

220   DEF FNM(F) = SQR(A + B)/SQR(A − B)

Reference may be made to variables other than the dummy variable in the definition of a user-defined function. In the following sequence of statements:

230   DEF FNH(I) = A*I*I + B*I + C
240   DATA 2,3,4,5
250   READ A,B,C,D
260   LET R = FNH(D)

R would contain the value (50 + 15 + 4) = 69 since the current values of the variables A,B,C used in the definition are applied in the evaluation of the function when called. The use of variables other than the dummy variable in the function definition can diminish one of the limitations of this technique − the restriction of the argument to a single expression.

The RND Function

There is a growing number of digital computer applications (such as the simulation of the behaviour of particles in a nuclear reactor) where situations involving randomness are encountered. Such simulations range from imitation of the behaviour of dice and roulette wheels to the simulation of full-scale nuclear wars. Much ingenuity has been applied to computer programs which produce pseudo-random numbers. (With truly random numbers the same series of numbers could never be produced repeatedly which would make programs difficult to debug.) The random numbers obtained by such programs satisfy such tests of randomness as the gap test which ensures that the same digit does not occur too often.

The standard BASIC function RND(X) selects a random number between 0 and 1 using a well-tested program for the generation of pseudo-random numbers. The statement:

270   LET K = RND(1)

would store one of these numbers in the variable K.

The sequence of statements:

```
280  FOR T = 1 TO 10
290  LET B(T) = RND(1)
300  PRINT B(T)
310  NEXT T
```

would store 10 random numbers between 0 and 1 in B(1) to B(10) and (on one computer) would print:

| .2435041 | .2998482 | .6075527 | .9466811 | .2121133 |
| .7525509 | .6062854 | .8647548 | .7319596 | .6089648 |

The argument used after RND varies considerably and you should consult the appropriate computer manufacturer's programming manual. On the IBM System 3 no argument is needed; on Computer Technology Mod 1 and PDP 11 an argument must be stated but its value is immaterial. In Honeywell BASIC, on the other hand, a positive number should be used in the first RND call and zero thereafter. Whenever the same positive number is used for initialisation, the same series of pseudo-random numbers ensues. In this book, 1 will be used as the argument of RND throughout the text.

If it is desired to repeat a program using a different set of random numbers you should consult your manufacturer's programming manual as to the appropriate technique to adopt since the same sequence of numbers is always repeated unless some alteration is made.

One method of starting at a different point in generating random numbers each time the program is run is to input a variable which will determine how many successive generations of numbers are to be ignored, e.g.

```
320  PRINT "TYPE HOW MANY RANDOMS TO BE
                                    IGNORED"
330  INPUT J
340  FOR I = 1 TO J
350  LET A = RND(1)
360  NEXT I
```

Often random numbers in a range other than between 0 and 1 are required. The following example uses the same computer as statements 280—310 in this chapter to print 20 random digits between 0 and 9. The resulting print out is also shown.

Functions and Subroutines

```
370    DIM B(20)
380    FOR T = 1 TO 20
390    LET X = RND(1')
400    REM CONVERTS TO RANGE 0-9
410    LET B(T) = INT(10* X)
420    PRINT B(T)
430    NEXT T
```

2	2	8	9	2
7	6	8	7	6
0	9	9	1	8
7	7	4	1	8

If you wish to simulate tossing a coin the appropriate statement will give either 0 or 1 with a probability of .5:

```
440    LET C = INT(RND(1) + .5)
```

If you wish to simulate the casting of an unbiased die with 6 equiprobable outcomes the appropriate statement would be:

```
450    LET D = INT(6*RND(1)) + 1
```

The following program shows the use of the RND function in the calculation of π. *Figure 9.1* shows a square enclosing the quadrant of a

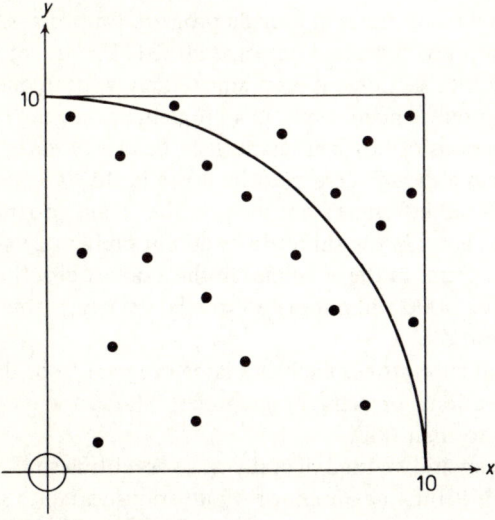

Figure 9.1 Square enclosing the quadrant of a circle of radius 10 units

circle of radius 10 units. Each point (x,y) is represented by a pair of random coordinates in the range 0–10. j records the total number of points generated and k records the number of points which lie on or within the boundary of the circle. Then (if enough points are taken)

$$\frac{j}{k} \simeq \frac{1}{\frac{1}{4}\pi}$$

so that $4k/j$ gives an approximation to π. The program uses 5000 points.

```
460   LET K = 0
470   FOR J = 1 TO 5000
480   LET X = INT(10*RND(1))
490   LET Y = INT(10*RND(1))
500   REM TESTS IF WITHIN QUADRANT
510   IF X↑2 + Y↑2 > 100 THEN 530
520   LET K = K + 1
530   NEXT J
540   PRINT "PI = ",4*K/J
99999 END
```

Subroutines

The concept of a subroutine as a self-contained set of statements which could be used many times in a single program for processes which are often required was discussed on pages 30–31. The use of subroutines saves effort since sections of program are only written once although they can be used as many times in a program as they are called or invoked. Sections of other programs may be incorporated in a program as subroutines although care must be taken in BASIC to ensure that the line numbers are different from those in the calling program and that the variable names in the subroutines do not obliterate values stored in the main program. In the examples in this book subroutines will use line numbers from 6000 and numbered variables starting from Z9. Arrays will start from Z.

The use of subroutines enables a large program to be divided into self-contained sections for many programmers who can work on a section appropriate to their skill.

Remarks should be used liberally in a subroutine so that a user other than yourself is fully cognisant of what various variables should contain on entry to the subroutine and in what variables the results will appear.

Functions and Subroutines

A user-defined function can be considered as a subroutine yet it has the great disadvantage of being limited to a single line. This excludes processes of any complexity and allows no branching or IF statements which can be essential for ensuring that the argument is suitable for the subroutine. The limitation of the argument of a user-defined function to a single dummy variable excludes the use of these functions for such processes as calculating the mean of an array where the lower bound and number of elements in the array would have to be defined on entrance to the function.

A subroutine is written as an ordinary sequence of statements. It is invoked by the GOSUB statement of the form:

    GOSUB line-number

In the subroutine itself control is transferred to the *line number* after the initiating GOSUB statement by a RETURN statement which just has the form:

    RETURN

The subroutine is not obeyed in the part of the program where it is written — only when it is invoked (this is similar to a user-defined function which is only obeyed when it appears in a statement and is not obeyed in the DEF statement).

The following example will clarify the above remarks. Three numbers are read and their factorials calculated.

```
 550   (Data list)
 560   FOR K = 1 TO 3
 570   READ A(K)
 580   LET Z9 = A(K)
 590   REM SUBROUTINE ENTERED
 600   GOSUB 6000
 610   PRINT "FACTORIAL OF", A(K), "IS", Z8
 620   NEXT K
 630   STOP
6000   LET Z8 = Z9
6010   IF   Z8 = 1 THEN 6060
6020   FOR Z7 = Z8 − 1 TO 1 STEP − 1
6030   LET Z8 = Z8 * Z7
6040   NEXT Z7
6050   REM END OF FACTORIAL.ANSWER IN Z8
```

```
6060    RETURN
99999   END
```

Subroutines should be written before the END statement and will not be compiled if they are after it. The STOP statement in line 630 prevents the subroutine being obeyed without being invoked by a GOSUB statement. Care should always be taken to ensure that a subroutine is only entered by a GOSUB, otherwise there is no control as to the point in the program where the RETURN statement would lead it.

No reference should be made in a subroutine by a GO TO or IF statement to line numbers external to it since its usefulness would be limited to a single program. Any DEF or DIM statement within a subroutine will apply throughout any program where it is used.

The RETURN statement need not be the final statement in a subroutine. It can be used at any point in the subroutine where it is desired to return to the instruction after the GOSUB which invoked it. The following program shows this facility of using more than one RETURN as well as the use of a subroutine for a data processing rather than a mathematical task. The subroutine ensures that the output is split into pages every 60 lines and prints a page heading.

```
640    REM SETS LINE COUNT INITIALLY
650    LET Z9 = 1
660    REM SETS INITIAL PAGE COUNT
670    LET Z8 = 0
680    REM PRINTS HEADING FOR FIRST PAGE
690    GOSUB 6100
700    FOR N = 1 TO 3000
710    PRINT N,N *N,N ↑3, 1/N,SQR(N)
720    GOSUB 6100
730    NEXT N
740    STOP
750    REM SUBROUTINE PAGE
6100   REM Z9 COUNTS LINES, Z8 COUNTS PAGES
6110   IF Z8 = 0 THEN 6200
6120   REM ABOVE TEST FOR INITIAL PAGE PRINT
6130   LET Z9 = Z9 + 1
6140   REM ABOVE AUGMENTS LINE COUNT
6150   IF Z9 > 61 THEN 6180
6160   REM NEW HEADING NOT YET NEEDED
6170   RETURN
```

Functions and Subroutines 103

```
6180   LET Z9 = 1
6190   REM SETS LINE COUNT TO 1
6200   LET Z8 = Z8 + 1
6210   REM ABOVE AUGMENTS PAGE NUMBER
6220   PRINT "– – – – – – PAGE",Z8"– – – – – – –"
6230   PRINT "NUMBER", "SQUARE","CUBE",
                            "RECIPROCAL","SQUARE ROOT"
6240   RETURN
99999  END
```

Subroutines can be nested so that one subroutine can invoke another which may be textually either before or after it. Care should be taken with variable names, and in transferring a subroutine of this type all subroutines it invokes will have to be transferred. Sometimes there is a limitation on the number of subroutines which can be nested – Honeywell BASIC only allows eight GOSUBS to be executed before a RETURN is executed.

The following example shows one subroutine calling another. The factorial subroutine calls a subroutine which ensures that only suitable numbers are processed.

```
760    (Data list)
770    FOR K = 1 TO 3
780    READ A(K)
790    LET Z9 = A(K)
800    GOSUB 6250
810    PRINT "FACTORIAL OF", A(K), "IS", Z8
820    NEXT K
830    STOP
840    REM START OF SUBROUTINES
6250   LET Z8 = Z9
6260   REM CALLS INPUT CHECK SUBROUTINE
6270   GOSUB 7000
6280   IF Z8 <= 1 THEN 6330
6290   FOR Z7 = Z8 – 1 TO 1 STEP – 1
6300   LET Z8 = Z8 *Z7
6310   NEXT Z7
6320   REM END OF FACTORIAL. ANSWER IN Z8
6330   RETURN
6340   REM  INPUT CHECK STARTS BELOW
7000   IF Z8 < 1 THEN 7040
```

```
7010    IF Z8 > 10 THEN 7040
7020    IF Z8 – INT(Z8) > 0 THEN 7040
7030    RETURN
7040    LET Z8 = 0
7050    REM PUTS RESULT TO ZERO IF INPUT ERROR
7060    RETURN
99999   END
```

Most versions of BASIC do not allow a subroutine to invoke itself (recursion) so this technique, elegant though it is, should be avoided (unless you are working on the PDP 11 computer).

Exercises 9.1

1. Write functions to perform the following operations and incorporate them in a program to process three items from a data list and one input number.

   a. Log to base 10.
   b. Tangent from argument in degrees.
   c. Area of circle from radius.
   d. Conversion of an angle in degrees to radians.
   e. Rounding of positive numbers so that 1.5 becomes 2.
   f. Cube root.

2. Simulate 100 throws of a dice and print the number of times each face appears.

3. Simulate the dealing of a hand of 13 cards from a single pack and print the hand.

4. A roulette wheel is numbered 0–36 (ignore 0!). Simulate 1000 spins of the wheel and print out the number of times you find Pair (evens), Impair (odd), Manque (1–18) and Passe (19–36).

5. Write subroutines to find

   a. the maximum
   b. the minimum

   of an array of numbers and use them in a program to read 10 numbers and print out the maximum and minimum.

Functions and Subroutines

6. Write a subroutine to convert a number in radians to an angle in degrees, minutes and seconds and use it in a program to input 10 numbers and print out their converted values.

7. Write and use a subroutine to solve the general quadratic $ax^2 + bx + c = 0$ using the formula method.

8. Write and use a subroutine to print out the factors of any positive integer less than 100.

Chapter 10

FURTHER PRINTING FACILITIES AND CHARACTER MANIPULATION

The output which you have been able to obtain on your terminal typewriter has up to now been restricted to printing your results in rigidly defined print zones. This is advantageous when dealing with tabular data where not more than five columns are required. The columns are automatically spaced under the appropriate headings by the use of the PRINT statement to which you are accustomed. If however you have to print data which occupies more character positions than are permitted in the print zone or wish to print more columns than the number of print zones (often 5) the printing format you have been hitherto utilising is unsatisfactory.

The print zones can be ignored if the commas in a PRINT statement are replaced by semicolons. Using this technique a smaller number of spaces is used for each numeric value. The exact size of this number, or print field, varies with different computers. Common print fields using semicolons are:

      6 spaces   1—3 digit numbers
      9 spaces   4—6 digit numbers
     12 spaces   7—9 digit numbers

No space is inserted between characters in quotation marks in a PRINT statement if they are separated by a semicolon. The contrast between using a comma and using a semicolon is demonstrated in the following examples:

```
100   DATA 7,70,700 7000,70000
110   READ A,B,C,D,E
120   PRINT A,B,C,D,E
130   PRINT A;B;C;D;E
140   PRINT "THIS","IS","AN","EXAMPLE"
150   PRINT "THIS";"IS";"AN";"EXAMPLE"
```

Further Printing Facilities and Character Manipulation 107

which would produce output:

```
7              70             700            7000           70000
7       70     700    7000           70000
THIS           IS                    AN             EXAMPLE
THISISANEXAMPLE
```

          160   PRINT "14 ";"JUNE ";"1972"

would print:

14 JUNE 1972

In a similar manner to the comma format, if the printing of the data in the print list would occupy more character positions than are available it is usual for the typewriter to continue automatically to the next line.

If you wish to print out values with a decimal fractional part it is more elegant to use the comma format where possible so that the decimal points are automatically aligned under each other. If you wish to print fractions in more fields than the number of print zones allows then you will have to use the semicolon format and calculate yourself how to ensure point alignment.

The semicolon format is especially useful for printing an explanation and a numeric value on the same line. The long gap which often occurs using the comma format is eliminated since no spaces are left after the printing of a message terminated by a semicolon and the next print field. The output from the following sequence of statements illustrates this:

          170   DATA 800000,700000,600000
          180   READ A,B,C
          190   LET M = (A+B+C)/3
          200   PRINT "MEAN =",M
          210   PRINT "MEAN =";M

```
MEAN =          700000
MEAN =700000
```

If you end a PRINT statement with either a comma or a semicolon the next PRINT statement will continue printing on the same line. The following example:

          220   DATA 7,8,9,10
          230   READ T,U,V,W
          240   PRINT T,U,

```
        250  PRINT V,W
        260  PRINT T; U;
        270  PRINT V; W;
```
would produce output:

```
7               8               9               10
7       8       9       10
```

Semicolon and comma formats can be mixed in a single print statement. The output from the following example shows the effect (the variables T–W have the values given to them in statement 230):

```
        280  PRINT "DATA IS",T;U,V;W
```

```
DATA IS         7       8               9       10
```

Many versions of BASIC include the TAB function which can be included inside a PRINT statement. The form is:

    TAB(integer expression)

The integer expression represents the number of a character position counting from the left-hand margin. The effect of the TAB function is to move the typewriter head to the right to the appropriate character position. The statement (using the data values above):

```
        290  PRINT  TAB(8);T; TAB(20);U
```

would produce output:

```
        7           8
```

The semicolon and comma formats override the TAB function so that the argument must be greater than the number of spaces which would normally be provided. Tabbing to the next line or to a character position less than the one already reached in printing should be avoided as different effects occur with different systems.

Using the TAB function you can exercise great control over the spacing of output across the page. It can be useful in alignment if you are using the semicolon printing format.

Character Manipulation

So far you have not been able to store alphanumeric characters but have only been able to use them in literal messages such as "TODAY IS

Further Printing Facilities and Character Manipulation 109

THURSDAY". You have not been able to input characters from data lists or from the keyboard and have not been able to do any comparison or sorting of input other than numbers.

Most versions of BASIC contain facilities for the input and manipulation of non-numeric information. There is a growing use of computer facilities for character work such as textual analysis although this usually would need different input facilities from the entry of characters on a data-list or from the keyboard and would also require the characters to be stored on magnetic tape or disc files. It is useful, however, in many programs to be able to do some manipulations with characters. When you did exercise 3 of the last chapter you may have felt the lack of this facility.

If you are working in a batch-processing mode with punched input it is possible to do some refined editing of texts with regard to paging and justification and to output the result on paper tape for reproduction on a teletype which can be controlled by paper tape, if character manipulation techniques are available in a computer language. You can also print approximate graphs and histograms on the terminal typewriter. These graphs will naturally not have the mathematical precision and accuracy which would be obtained from using a graph-plotter but for more general purposes you can produce useful graphs at the terminal typewriter using the BASIC character manipulation facilities. Applications with generative grammars in formal linguistics can be performed using the available BASIC character facilities.

Characters in BASIC are treated as being contained in "strings". A string may be defined as a sequence of characters treated as a unit. You have already encountered strings in the PRINT statement. In the statement:

    100   PRINT "JULIA ALISON SANDERSON"

the characters between quotes are a string. A string can contain the characters in the character set of the computer you are using. A space is a character so the above string contains 22 characters. A string can consist of only one character, e.g. "*". It is best to avoid the use of quotation marks within a string. The quotation marks themselves are not part of a string. Even though their use in string demarcation is in some circumstances optional in some BASIC dialects, it is best always to use them to mark the beginning and end of a character string. Naturally the numeric characters 0–9 can be part of a string. In their character form they are stored in a different way inside a string to their form used when performing computations. The string form should never be used for arithmetic. A string is held inside a string variable. A string variable consists of one of the letters A–Z followed by a dollar sign so that A$, E$ and X$ are all valid string variables. A subscripted variable of *one* dimension can also be used to store a string. This would comprise a string variable followed by a subscript. String arrays have to be declared in a DIM statement and can be mixed in this declaration with numerical arrays, e.g.

    300   DIM E(40),B$(15),Y(5,6),F$(25)

Each item or element in a string array contains a whole string which can be a single character.

The number of characters which it is permitted to hold in a string variable varies from one computer to another and the appropriate programming manual should be consulted. For many of the computers you are likely to encounter this information is supplied in Chapter 12. This book will assume that a string variable can contain a maximum of 15 characters.

Characters can be stored in a string variable by the use of DATA and READ statements. The following sequence of statements:

    310   DATA 6,"ENIGMA",19.5
    320   READ V,M$
    330   DATA "VARIATIONS"
    340   READ Q
    350   READ V$

would place ENIGMA in M$ and VARIATIONS in V$.

If a string is longer than the maximum number of characters allowed in a string variable it must be split up into units according to the required maximum (in our case 15 characters). The following example shows this technique:

    360   DATA "EDWARD ELGAR WA","S BORN IN WORCE",
                                         "STERSHIRE."

If this was followed by the statements:

    370   READ A$,B$,C$
    380   PRINT A$;B$;C$

The output:

Further Printing Facilities and Character Manipulation 111

EDWARD ELGAR WAS BORN IN WORCESTERSHIRE.

would be produced.

You must be careful not to become confused in reading mixed data lists so that you attempt to store a string in a non-string variable (or vice versa). This will lead to a program error since strings and numbers from data lists are stored in separate data pools. Especial care is needed when using RESTORE with long mixed data lists since it is easy for some confusion to arise here. The above example also shows the use of the PRINT statement with string variables. The semicolon format puts the strings together with no extra spaces added. The effect of printing string variables with the comma format would, in the following sequence of statements:

```
390   DATA "GERARD","MANLEY","HOPKINS","."
400   READ D$,E$,F$,G$
410   PRINT D$,E$,F$,G$
```

produce output as:

GERARD   MANLEY   HOPKINS

String and ordinary variables can be intermixed in a PRINT statement as in the following example:

```
420   LET A = 3
430   DATA "RESULT","="
440   READ X$,Y$
450   FOR N = 1 TO 3
460   PRINT X$;N;Y$;A↑N
470   NEXT N
```

Output would be produced as:

RESULT1   = 3
RESULT2   = 9
RESULT3   = 27

The INPUT statement can be used to enter strings directly from the terminal typewriter keyboard. A practical example of this technique is shown in statement 530 in this chapter.

Strings can also be introduced into string variables by the use of the LET statement. This can be used either to store one variable in another, e.g.

480   LET R$ = H$

or to store a string in a variable, e.g.

490   LET K$ = "WINDFLOWER"

Any would-be arithmetic expressions or attempts at concatenation of strings in a LET statement are not allowed, so that expressions of the type:

500   LET X$ = "A" + D$

are illegal. (Some compilers would allow such a useful facility for linguistic work and also allow the user to define string functions.)

You cannot perform any serious work with strings unless you have the facility of being able to compare two strings. This is useful for checking input strings, for sorting string information into order and for identifying a string. Using the IF statement you may compare strings using the same six relational operators as you have used for numeric information. To make such comparisons you will need to ascertain the collation sequence used by the computer on which you are working. This will give the exact order in which every element of the character set is sequenced.

A common collation sequence, and one which will be followed in this book is (in ascending order):

space ! " $ % & ' ( ) * + , − . / 0–9 : ; < = > ? A–Z

In any scheme A<Z and 0<9. Spaces at the end of a string (sometimes called "trailing blanks") are ignored in a comparison so that "ANASTASIA" and "ANASTASIA   " would be accounted equivalent.

The string interpretations of the six relational operators are:

=		The strings are equivalent.
<>		The strings are not equivalent.
X$ < Y$		The string X$ occurs before the string Y$ in alphabetical sequence.
X$ <= Y$		The string X$ is equivalent to or occurs before the string Y$ in alphabetical sequence.
X$ > Y$		The string X$ occurs after the string Y$ in alphabetical sequence.
X$ >= Y$		The string X$ is equivalent to or occurs after the string Y$ in alphabetical sequence.

Further Printing Facilities and Character Manipulation

String variables or strings can be used in the IF statement. The following sequence of statements shows the use of the IF statement in connection with the identification of string input:

```
510   PRINT "DO YOU WISH TO CONTINUE ?"
520   PRINT " TYPE YES OR NO "
530   INPUT G$
540   IF G$ = "NO" THEN 99999
550   (rest of program)
```

If two strings of different lengths are being compared, one string and the corresponding part of the other string are used. If this comparison results in equivalence the former string is considered the shorter, so that in the following sequence of statements 2 is printed:

```
560   DATA "ALEXANDRA","ALEX"
570   IF X$>K$ THEN 610
590   PRINT "1"
600   STOP
610   PRINT "2"
```

You will have to ascertain the position of "space" in the collating sequence of the system you are using to ensure whether "ABBEY WOOD" is counted as greater or less than "ABBEYFIELD" if you wish to use the letter-by-letter rather than the word-by-word sorting technique.

String array elements are useful for storing words of a sentence. The following example shows the input of a simple sentence with a full stop as a string by itself to mark its end. Each word is stored in an array element.

```
620   (Data list)
630   REM ALLOWS SPACE FOR THE LONGEST
                                       SENTENCE
640   DIM M$(30)
650   LET K = 1
660   READ M$(K)
670   IF M$(K) = "." THEN 700
680   LET K = K + 1
690   GO TO 660
700   STOP
```

Exercises 10.1

1. Read in five words from a data list, sort them and print them in alphabetical order.

2. Read from a data list a sentence of not more than 30 words which ends with a full stop as a string in itself. Store the sentence in elements of a string array and print out the number of words.

3. Simulate the drawing of 10 cards at random from a pack and print the full descriptions of the cards drawn.

4. A positive integer of not more than six digits is input at the keyboard character by character and terminated by an asterisk. Print the number, its square and its square root.

5. Read 10 integers (smaller than 30) and by the side of each integer print a bar-chart (with +s) showing the value of each number, e.g.

    7 +++++++

6. Read a number and print in words the remainder when divided by 11.

Chapter 11

MATRIX INSTRUCTIONS

The majority of versions of BASIC have powerful statements for matrix manipulation which are not found in the usual mathematical high-level languages, FORTRAN and ALGOL 60. You have already seen some examples of matrix manipulation in Chapter 8 where the FOR statement was used. The BASIC matrix statements save the programmer time in writing nested FOR statements and (in some cases) save him the effort of writing complicated mathematical algorithms. These statements are also of use to the non-mathematician who wishes to handle large blocks of data in tabular form.

You will remember that usually a matrix is declared in a DIM statement. This practice should be followed if you are going to use the BASIC matrix instructions.

Given below are the BASIC matrix instructions which are usually found in most systems. Detailed explanations of some of them will be given later in the chapter. A matrix is described by its initial letter. (It is assumed that no row or column has a subscript 0: subscript 0 is better avoided.) Matrices are referred to below as A,B,C.

MAT READ A,B,C	reads from a data list into matrices A,B,C.
MAT INPUT A,B,C	awaits input from the terminal typewriter to fill matrices A,B,C.
MAT PRINT A,B,C	prints the matrices A,B,C row by row.
MAT A = B	stores matrix B in A.
MAT A = B + C	adds two matrices.
MAT A = B − C	subtracts two matrices.
MAT A = B*C	multiplies two matrices according to the rules of *matrix* multiplication.
MAT A = TRN(B)	puts the transpose of B in A.
MAT A = ZER	sets all elements of A to zero.

MAT A = CON	sets all elements of A to one.
MAT A = (K)*B	multiplies all elements of B by a scalar constant K.
MAT A = IDN	sets up A as an identity matrix with ones in the leading diagonal and zeros elsewhere.
MAT A = INV(B)	sets A to the inverse of matrix B.

MAT READ is useful in many data processing applications for reading tables of data with a single statement. In the majority of systems the data are read in row by row but your computer manufacturer's programming manual should be consulted on this point.

The power and economy of the above instruction can be demonstrated by comparing the following sequence of statements with the sequence 940–1020 on page 93 where the same problem of filling a 6 by 8 matrix from a data list was solved by the use of two FOR statements.

```
100   DATA (24 numbers)
110   DATA (24 numbers)
120   DIM D(6, 8)
130   MAT READ D
```

A MAT READ statement will handle one or several matrices. The matrices in a single MAT READ statement need not have the same dimensions. In most versions of BASIC the MAT READ facility can be used as an economic method of reading in lists. If you wish to do this you must define a matrix with one row and the same number of columns as there are list elements. The following sequence reads 48 items from a data list and stores them in $F(1,1)$ to $F(1,48)$.

```
140   DIM F(1,48)
150   MAT READ F
```

The RESTORE statement can be used in the usual manner in conjunction with MAT READ.

MAT INPUT works in a similar manner to MAT READ and fills a matrix or matrices from the terminal typewriter input.

MAT PRINT is also useful in data processing when you wish to print tables. Both the comma and semicolon print formats can be used. The following example demonstrates these formats used in conjunction with a MAT READ statement.

Matrix Instructions 117

```
160   DIM G(2,3),H (3,4)
170   DATA 1,2,3,4,5,6,12,11,10,9,8,7,6,5,4,3,2,1
180   MAT READ G,H
190   PRINT "MATRIX G"
200   MAT PRINT G;
210   PRINT "MATRIX H"
220   MAT PRINT H
```

The output from the sequence of statements is given below.

```
MATRIX G
1       2       3
4       5       6
MATRIX H
12              11              10              9
8               7               6               5
4               3               2               1
```

The comma is optional after a single matrix in a MAT PRINT or after the last matrix name in the statement if it is wanted to print in the usual print zones. The semicolon is never implicit. Commas and semicolons can be mixed in the same MAT PRINT statement. The statement can also be used for printing lists if they are suitably dimensioned with a row number of 1. If a row is larger than the print-line, printing of the elements will continue on the next row. This possibility can often be avoided by the use of the semicolon format.

If you use the replacement statement of the form:

```
230   MAT X = P
```

you must be sure that the matrices are of the same dimensions. This statement can be useful for making copies of tables in the computer store.

The matrix add and subtract statements are useful in some data processing applications such as the addition of all elements of two tables of the same size. Care should always be taken to ensure that the matrices which can appear in a matrix add or subtract statement have identical dimensions. The same matrix can appear on both sides of the equals sign so that:

```
240   MAT X = Y + K
250   MAT V = V − L
```

are acceptable statements. Only one matrix arithmetic operation can be performed in a statement so an instruction of the type:

    260   MAT J = K + L − P

is invalid.

The following example adds and subtracts two matrices with 3 rows and 4 columns and prints the results.

```
270   DIM T(3,4), U(3,4),V(3,4), W(3,4)
280   DATA 1,2,3,4,5,6,7,8,9,10,11,12,13,14,15,16,17,18
290   DATA 19, 20, 21, 22, 23, 24
300   MAT READ T,U
310   MAT V = T + U
320   MAT W = U − T
330   PRINT "SUM"
340   MAT PRINT V
350   PRINT "DIFFERENCE"
360   MAT PRINT W
```

From the output below it will be observed that matrix V consists of the sum of corresponding elements and matrix W consists of their difference.

SUM
14	16	18	20
22	24	26	28
30	32	34	36

DIFFERENCE
12	12	12	12
12	12	12	12
12	12	12	12

The matrix multiply statement does *not* multiply corresponding elements. The statement uses the rules of matrix multiplication and should not be used for data processing work. This statement is only of interest to programmers with a knowledge of matrix arithmetic.

Care should be taken to see that the matrices are multiplied in the desired order since in general A*B is not equal to B*A.

In the statement:

    370   MAT Y = G*K

Matrix Instructions

the number of rows of K must equal the number of columns of G. The resulting matrix Y will have the number of rows of G and columns of K. Matrices G and K need not be of the same order or square if the above is true. The matrix on the left of the equals sign cannot appear on the right of it since elements are stored as soon as they are calculated so that one of the multiplier matrices would be destroyed in its original form.

The transpose statement changes rows for columns and can be considered as having some occasional uses in data processing and table manipulation applications. The sizes of the matrices have to be defined so that in the statement:

MAT A = TRN(B)

if A is an m by n matrix then B is n by m. $A(m,n)$ is set equal to $B(n,m)$ for all values of m,n. The following example demonstrates the transpose statement:

```
380   DATA 1,2,3,4,5,6,7,8,9,10,11,12
390   DIM H(4,3),Q (3,4)
400   MAT READ H
410   MAT Q = TRN(H)
420   PRINT "ORIGINAL MATRIX H"
430   MAT PRINT H
440   PRINT "TRANSPOSE Q"
450   MAT PRINT Q
```

ORIGINAL MATRIX H

1	2	3
4	5	6
7	8	9
10	11	12

TRANSPOSE Q

1	4	7	10
2	5	8	11
3	6	9	12

The ZER function sets all elements to zero and the CON sets all elements to 1. The CON function can be used in conjunction with the scalar multiplication statement to set all elements of a matrix to a desired value.

The form of the scalar multiplication statement is:

MAT A = (K)* B

where A and B are matrices of the same dimensions and K is a variable, constant or arithmetic expression by which it is desired to multiply all elements of B. The following statements show the CON and scalar multiplication instructions:

```
460   DIM D(3,2),M(3,2)
470   MAT D = CON
480   MAT M = (7)*D
490   PRINT "MATRIX D"
500   MAT PRINT D
510   PRINT "MATRIX M"
520   MAT PRINT M
```

MATRIX D
1   1
1   1
1   1
MATRIX M
7   7
7   7
7   7

The IDN function sets every element on the leading diagonal of a matrix to 1 and the rest of the elements to zero. The matrix must be defined as a square matrix. Any previous values of the elements are destroyed.

The INV function is useful in solving simultaneous linear equations. It should only be used with square matrices. Care should be taken in using this function since there are cases where the inverse of a matrix will not exist (such as the case where one row is a multiple of another). In the statement:

MAT V = INV(P)

the same matrix cannot (in most versions of BASIC) appear on both sides of the equals sign.

Chapter 12

VERSIONS OF BASIC

Frequent reference has been made in previous chapters to the availability of some features (such as the multiple assignment statement) which are not common to the implementations of BASIC on all computers. BASIC has not been rigorously defined like ALGOL and has not been standardised by the American National Standards Institution or similar body. Therefore many variations have been improvised on the basic theme of the original language since its inception in 1965.

In addition to the inevitable variations between computers, such as the range of numbers which can be expressed, BASIC compilers have introduced extensions which are unique to specific types of computer. These extensions enhance the power of the language but unfortunately create problems when you wish to run your program on another computer.

This book has dealt with the common subset of BASIC which can be found in all implementations. The only slight exceptions to this rule are the discussion of the multiple assignment statement and the ON GO TO statement but these are implemented on the great majority of computers with BASIC compilers. There are some versions of BASIC more common in the U.S.A. than in Britain which do not have any character handling statements. Yet it is considered that BASIC described in the previous chapters does not include facilities which are not possessed by the types of computer you are most likely to use. Some of the features which have been added to the language in various implementations are:

The ability to omit LET in an assignment statement.
Multiple statements on a line.
Logical operators.
File procedures.
Character functions.

The following table shows some slight variations in implementation of common features of BASIC which are found on some computers.

Some Variants of BASIC

	Burroughs B5500	CDC Intercom 1	Computer Technology Mod 1	Honeywell Time-Sharing	IBM Call/360	IBM System 3	ICL 1900 Series	PDP11 RSTS-11 BASIC-PLUS	Univac 1108 Exec 8
Line Format									
Maximum number of characters in program line	72	75	10	72	255	243	75	255	75
Maximum line number	9999	99999	32767	32767	99999	9999	99999	32767	99999
Standard printout	4 zones of 15 print positions: 1 of 12	5 zones of 15 print positions	5 zones of 15 print positions	5 zones of 13 print positions	4 zones of 18 print positions	WIDTH command	5 zones of 15 print positions	5 zones of 14 print positions	5 zones of 15 print positions
Numeric Variables									
Variable initialise to zero?	Yes	Yes	No	Yes	Yes	Yes	Yes	Yes	Yes
First element of arrays	1	0	1	0	1	1	0	0	0
Character Variables									
Form	A$	None	A$	A$	A$	A$	A$ or A£	A$	A$
Maximum size of string contained in a variable (number of characters)	15	–	127	Any length	18	18	15	Any length	60
Statement Facilities									
Multiple assignment statement?	Yes	Yes	Yes	No	Yes	Yes	Yes	Yes	Yes
ON GO TO?	Yes	No	Yes	Yes	Yes	Yes	Yes	Yes	Yes

Chapter 13

FROM BASIC TO FORTRAN

All the main features of the BASIC language have now been discussed. You may find that the particular version of BASIC which you use in your installation contains more elegant and sophisticated variants than the statements discussed in previous chapters so that you can have recourse to greater facilities than many users of BASIC. There is no doubt however that even the essential BASIC is a very versatile language for the solution of problems on a computer terminal.

Nevertheless there are certain features of BASIC which appear deficient when compared with FORTRAN, ALGOL or PL/I.

The control over printed format in BASIC is severely limited since the language was designed primarily for the output of a relatively small series of numbers on a terminal typewriter. If you want more ambitious output statements, such as are often essential in information processing applications, you will find the output system of FORTRAN more flexible and relevant to your needs. Some versions of BASIC (such as IBM System 3) incorporate some FORTRAN features as extensions.

The input statements of BASIC are relatively unsophisticated for reading a mass of data for statistical analysis from punched cards or paper tape. There are data file handling features in some versions of BASIC but there is little uniformity in the way data files are manipulated in versions for different computers. The FORTRAN input system provides useful facilities for handling large amounts of punched data.

You may have found the lack of mnemonic variable names tiresome and productive of more lines of remarks than would be used if BASIC contained mnemonic features. It is unlikely that at this stage you will have found the need for more than 234 variable names or 26 arrays but in certain circumstances the latter limitation could prove irksome. There are certain applications where the restriction of the number of subscripts to two could hamper a programmer. You may have found too that you needed at some points in your programs to use a function which could not be adequately defined in a single line or which needed more than a single argument. FORTRAN provides adequate facilities to transcend these limitations. You will remember that in Chapter 9 line numbers for subroutines were given with care so that a subroutine could be transferred from program to program. This would naturally not be possible if you wished to transfer a subroutine to a program which used the subroutine line numbers for other purposes. FORTRAN enables a subroutine to be written completely independently of any main program. This facility also allows you to duplicate variable names in a subroutine and any program to which it is attached.

To appreciate the full facilities of ANSI FORTRAN (the most powerful version of FORTRAN, formerly referred to as FORTRAN IV) it is necessary to study carefully the appropriate programming manual for your installation. FORTRAN was designed as a language based on punched card input and line-printer output although you may find an interactive version for the computer you use which will enable you to type FORTRAN programs statement by statement at a terminal. The rest of this chapter gives some simple rules for the quick translation of BASIC programs into FORTRAN. It is *not* intended to be a substitute for a detailed and thorough study of a FORTRAN manual and does not go into details about the use of FORTRAN statements. This chapter also does not discuss FORTRAN statements and directives (such as EQUIVALENCE) which have no parallel in BASIC. It is hoped that the rules listed below will enable you to translate your existing BASIC programs quickly into FORTRAN and will illustrate the general rules which will be described in your FORTRAN manual. In view of the great number of useful extant FORTRAN programs (such as the BMD series of biomedical statistical programs of the University of California) you may also find the rules useful in a study of a FORTRAN program.

It is felt that if the following steps are applied to a BASIC program the transition to FORTRAN will be quickly made. Only features common to most versions of BASIC will be discussed.

If you are not using an interactive version of FORTRAN it is most likely that you will be punching the program on punched cards. (There is considerable variation for different computers in the format of FORTRAN on paper tape.) The layout of FORTRAN statements on an 80 column punched card is described below.

Columns 1–5: statement number. Blanks and leading zeros are ignored.

From BASIC to FORTRAN

Column 6: left blank unless the card is a continuation card of a statement which occupies more than a single card. By convention it then contains the number of that card in the statement.

Columns 7–72: contain the FORTRAN statement. If a C is punched in column 1 the card is regarded as a comment or remarks card and columns 2–72 may be used for this purpose.

Columns 73–80: ignored by the compiler.

Steps for Translating a BASIC program into ANSI FORTRAN

1. Omit system commands or replace them by the appropriate FORTRAN system commands or job control cards.

2. If terminal FORTRAN is to be used line numbers will be needed for every statement. If batch-processing FORTRAN is to be used the only BASIC line numbers which will need to be kept are those in an IF-THEN or GO TO statement. Line numbers preceding a NEXT statement should be retained (*see* step 15).

3. Replace REM (if you are using batch-processing FORTRAN) by a C in column 1 of the card, followed by the appropriate remark. If you are using interactive FORTRAN consult your programming manual for the convention for the entry of comments or remarks.

4. Omit LET for all assignment statements.

5. Multiple assignment statements are not allowed in standard versions of FORTRAN so these will have to be replaced by several assignment statements, e.g.

$$\text{LET} \quad A = D = E = S = 175.1969$$

could be converted as:

$$A = 175.1969$$
$$D = A$$
$$E = A$$
$$S = A$$

6. If you have (unwisely) been using the assumption not common to all versions of BASIC that variables are all set to zero at the start of a program you will have to write FORTRAN statements to set all these to zero.

7. Standard versions of FORTRAN do not allow mixed integer and real types of numbers in the same assignment statement so you will

have to make appropriate alterations according to the form in which you wish the answer to be. The BASIC statement:

>   LET R = T + 7

could be converted as:

>   R = T + 7.0

8. In FORTRAN variable names with the initial letters I—N are used to contain integer quantities only and names beginning with other letters contain real quantities. These conventions are implicit in the language and can be overridden by type declarations of the form:

>   REAL list of variable names
>   INTEGER list of variable names

The following sequence of BASIC statements:

>   100   LET R = 10
>   110   LET I = −6
>   120   LET K = 2
>   130   LET Q1 = R + I − K

could be converted as:

>   INTEGER R,Q1
>   R = 10
>   I = −6
>   K = 2
>   Q1 = R + I − K

if the above variables *throughout the FORTRAN program* were never going to be used to store quantities with a decimal or fractional part. The same variable cannot be used at one time to contain integers and at another to contain real values on the same program.

To convert quantities from integer to real or floating point form the function FLOAT is used. This can convert an individual variable, e.g.

>   LET R = J + H

can be converted as:

>   R = FLOAT(J) + H

or an expression, e.g.

>   H = FLOAT(J*K + 3)

From BASIC to FORTRAN

There is an equivalent function IFIX which converts real quantities to integers and gives the largest integer $\leq$ the floating point quantity under conversion. The statement:

LET K = L + 7*H

can be converted as:

K = L + 7* IFIX(H)

9. The arithmetic operators in FORTRAN are identical to the BASIC operators with the exception of the exponentiation symbol. In FORTRAN this is written ** so that A↑4 would be expressed in FORTRAN as A**4.

10. Standard function names are identical in BASIC and FORTRAN with the exception of SQR which is written as SQRT. There is no RND function in FORTRAN.

11. Care should be taken with division of integer quantities which in FORTRAN always gives a result rounded towards zero. If you want to ensure a fractional answer when converting a statement such as:

LET K = I/4

you will have to use a technique such as:

AK = FLOAT(I)/ 4.0

(You can always convert an integer variable name to a real one by putting a letter in the range A–H,O–Z before it.)

12. The form of the GO TO statement is the same in both languages.

13. You will have to alter the form of the computed GO TO statement from

ON K GO TO 110, 120,9999

to

GO TO (110,120,9999),K

14. In the IF statement the FORTRAN relational operators and their BASIC equivalents are given below.

FORTRAN	BASIC
.EQ.	=
.NE.	<>
.LT.	<
.LE.	<=
.GT.	>
.GE.	>=

Instead of THEN statement number you will have to substitute GO TO statement number and you will have to enclose the comparison in parentheses. Some FORTRAN IF statements and their BASIC equivalents are shown below.

FORTRAN	BASIC
IF(B**2 .GE. E*C) GO TO 160	IF B↑2>=E*C THEN 160
IF(M .EQ. 17) GO TO 370	IF M = 17 THEN 370
IF(I .LT. J) GO TO 250	IF I < J THEN 250

15. The BASIC FOR statement is replaced by the FORTRAN DO statement with CONTINUE (optionally) taking the place of NEXT. Only integers and integer variables can be used in a standard FORTRAN DO statement (or DO loop as it is usually termed). A BASIC statment such as:

FOR T = A TO 8.5 STEP .5

could not easily be translated.

The form of the FORTRAN DO loop is DO number of last statement in loop controlled variable = initial value, terminal value, increment. The increment can be omitted when it is 1.

All three values on the right-hand side of = must be greater than zero at the time when the loop is executed. Therefore a BASIC statement such as:

FOR L = 10 TO 1 STEP −1

could not be converted to a DO loop. No assumptions should be made about the terminal value of the controlled variable on exit from a DO loop.

DO loops may be nested in a similar manner to FOR statements.

The following sequences of statements show the equivalent process in FORTRAN and BASIC.

FORTRAN			BASIC	
	DO 140	IH = 10,14,2	100	FOR H = 10 TO 14 STEP 2
		IA = IH −3	120	LET A = H − 3
		IR = IR + IA	130	LET R = R + A
140	CONTINUE		140	NEXT H
	DO 220	K = 1,M	200	FOR K = 1 TO M
		J = J + K	210	LET J = J + K
220	CONTINUE		220	NEXT K

From BASIC to FORTRAN 129

Since standard FORTRAN will only allow integers or integer variables in a DO statement the following BASIC statement:

FOR N = M↑3 − L TO ABS(I+J) STEP K−2

would have to be translated by such statements as:

```
         JA = M**3 − L
         JB = ABS(I+J)
         JC = K − 2
DO 47    N = JA,JB,JC
```

16. The equivalent statement in FORTRAN to DIM is DIMENSION which is *never* implicit and must always be used when you need to work with subscripted variables. Otherwise its use is the same as in BASIC. The BASIC statement:

DIM K(15), Y(7,5),E(20)

would be translated as:

DIMENSION K(15), Y(7,5),E(20)

Subscripts are assumed to start at 1 (unlike some versions of BASIC). If the first statement of a BASIC program was:

100   LET N(4) = 8

this would have to be modified in accordance with the rule that a subscripted variable cannot be used in a FORTRAN statement until it has been dimensioned, so that the equivalent FORTRAN statements could read:

DIMENSION N(10)
N(4) = 8

FORTRAN allows 3 dimensions in arrays but the third dimension will not be used if you are translating existing BASIC programs.

17. Subscripts in FORTRAN should always have exact integer values.

18. Subroutine procedures are very different. A FORTRAN subroutine is an independent segment of program or sequence of statements with its own line numbers and independent variable values. It is given a name and is invoked by CALL name of subroutine. The name must not be that of any variable, standard function or programmer defined function. Values are usually passed to and from subroutines by parameters or arguments which follow the subroutine name. The values are passed

back to the main program in the order of the parameters in the declaration. In the sequence of FORTRAN statements:

>   CALL AD4(A,K,M)
>   – – – – – – – –
>   – – – – – – – –
>   SUBROUTINE AD4(X,I,J)
>   – – – – – – – –
>   – – – – – – – –
>   X = 7.5
>   I = 1
>   J = −6
>   END

on return to the main program, A would have the value 7.5, K the value 1 and J the value −6. Often values input to a subroutine are expressions rather than variables so that only the results of computation are passed back to a variable in the main program. A subroutine has an END statement at the end of its text. RETURN is used at any point where you desire to return to the main program. A subroutine can call upon another subroutine.

The following sequence of statements shows the FORTRAN and BASIC versions of a subroutine and its invocation. This subroutine reads a quantity in millimetres and gives output values in metres, centimetres and millimetres.

```
              FORTRAN                              BASIC
       CALL METRE(MM,M,ICM,IMM)           GOSUB 800
       – – – – – – – – – – – – –          – – – – – –
       – – – – – – – – – – – – –          – – – – – –
       – – – – – – – – – – – – –          – – – – – –
       SUBROUTINE METRE(J,K,L,M)          – – – – – –
       K = J/1000                    800  LET K = J/1000
       L = J−1000*K                  810  LET L = J − 1000*K
       IF L .EQ. 0 GO TO 840         820  IF L = 0 THEN 840
       L = L/10                      830  LET L = L/10
   840 M = J−(1000*K + 10*L)         840  LET M = J − (1000*K+10*L
       RETURN                        850  RETURN
       END
```

From BASIC to FORTRAN

When the FORTRAN instructions return control to the main program, the metres will be stored in M, centimetres in ICM and millimetres in IMM. The input value in J is unchanged by the subroutine. M in the subroutine is completely independent of M in the main program.

There are a great many other facilities in a FORTRAN subroutine which are absent from a BASIC one but as these do not affect the conversion of a simple BASIC program to FORTRAN they will not be described here.

19. END is used in FORTRAN for the end of the text of the main program and for any subroutines. It is an instruction for the compiler only and cannot be used to halt execution of the program as it can in BASIC. STOP should always be used in FORTRAN for this purpose.

20. FORTRAN has the facility for defining functions analogous to the DEF statement in BASIC. The function name is written followed by parameters (more than one are allowed) and then the expression which computes the function. The function is not obeyed when written — only when invoked — and the variables can be considered dummy variables as in BASIC and have no effect on other variables of the same name. The following example shows the same function and its invocation in both FORTRAN and BASIC:

FORTRAN	BASIC
SND(A) = SIN(A*.017453)	100 DEF FNS(A) = SIN(A*.017453)
----------------	------------------
----------------	------------------
X = SND(P)	470 LET X = SND(P)

A FORTRAN function statement with multiple arguments or parameters could be:

SUM(A,B,C,D) = A+B+C+D

which could be invoked by such a statement as:

Y = 17.5 + SUM(P,ABS(F/Q), −15.4,T)

21. You can use the FORTRAN facility of writing a function as a separate segment if you want to use it throughout the program and not just in a single routine or segment. A function statement cannot be used outside the section of program in which it is written so that such a statement in the main program could not be invoked in a subroutine and vice versa. If it was desired to write the above function so that it was

available throughout the program it would be written separately with the title on a line to itself and a RETURN statement whenever it was wanted to return to the statement after the invocation. It is usual to define the type of function before its name, e.g.

```
REAL FUNCTION SND(A)
SND = SIN(A*.017453)
RETURN
END
```

You will see that the form is analagous to the subroutine procedure. You must always remember to see that the desired computed value is put into the function name before RETURN is made.

22. Character manipulation is best avoided by beginners to FORTRAN.

23. There are no matrix statements in FORTRAN.

24. There are great differences in the input and output facilities. Data for FORTRAN programs is often read from punched cards in the batch-processing mode. (The DATA statement in FORTRAN has a completely different use from the DATA statement in BASIC.) If you are working with interactive FORTRAN at a terminal your programming manual will inform you of the conventions for entering data at the terminal typewriter keyboard. This section is concerned with the reading of the punched cards. The format of the read statement is:

READ (device number, format number) input variable list

The device number refers to a particular input peripheral and will be supplied by your installation.

The format number refers to a format statement in the program which allows you to specify the manner in which you will present the input which is assumed to be on punched cards. (Your installation will supply details of any additional or special format requirements for punched paper tape or direct input from the terminal typewriter.)

A typical READ statement and accompanying format statement (which can occur at any point in the same segment of the program) could be:

```
        READ (10,7) J,K
     7  FORMAT (I5,I6)
```

This means that two integers (the I format) would be read from a card. The first integer, to be stored in J, would be punched in the first

From BASIC to FORTRAN

5 columns of the card, the second, to be stored in K, in the next 6 columns.

Each format statement refers to at least one card. You cannot read part of a card by one READ statement and then expect to read the rest of the card in another READ statement. Leading blanks are ignored but blanks in the middle of a number will cause trouble. If signs are punched they must be counted in the number of digits or field-width after I.

If all numbers in a card can be considered as having the same format a format statement such as:

   16   FORMAT (8I5)

can be used.

The F Format is used for reading quantities with a decimal part. The form is:

     F m.n

where m represents the number of digits in the whole field and n the number of digits in the decimal portion of the number. The decimal point is not usually punched. If it is, it overrides the number of decimal places requested in the F specification.

If the first 8 columns of a card were punched:

12345678

the sequence of statements:

     READ (10,5) A,X
   5   FORMAT (F3.1,F5.3)

would store 12.3 in A and 45.678 in X.

Negative signs are included in the field-width. F and I specifications can be mixed in the same format statement.

If you wish to indicate blank columns specially the X format can be used:

     5 X

would specify that the next 5 columns would be ignored.

If the first 20 columns of a card were punched:

123   −6789   9087   65

the following sequence of statements:

```
      READ (10,8) H,I,Y,M
    8 FORMAT (F3.1,2X,I5,2X,F4.2,2X,I2)
```
would store 12.3 in H, −6789 in I, 90.87 in Y and 65 in M.

/ in a format statement causes a new card to be used. The following sequence of statements would read the first 6 columns of two cards:

```
      READ (10,51) M,K
   51 FORMAT (I6/I6)
```

A whole array can be read with a single statement, e.g.

```
      DIMENSION A (20)
      READ (10,15) A
```

or by using a facility known as "an implied DO statement". Any number of these can appear in a single READ statement. The following sequence of statements reads a whole array of 10 elements:

```
      READ (10,17) (Y(N), N = 1,10)
   17 FORMAT (10(F3.2,2X))
```

Format statements are also used when outputing results. The form of the output statement is:

   WRITE (output device, format number) output variable list

The sequence of statements:

```
      WRITE (8,6) I,A,T,M
    6 FORMAT (I6,4X,F8.3,2X,F4.1,7X,I4)
```

could produce output as:

−12345   67.891   −4.2   17

A character position should be allowed for the sign and (in an F specification) for a decimal point. Each WRITE statement prints or types at least one line. / produces a new line so that n slashes will produce $n-1$ blank lines. The following format statement would print on 3 lines:

```
   89 FORMAT (I4/I6/F7.2)
```

In the F specification, the number is rounded on the last decimal position requested.

The H format is analagous to the PRINT "A STRING" feature in BASIC. The theoretical form is:

   nH

From BASIC to FORTRAN 135

and n characters after the H are output. In many versions of FORTRAN the first character after H (which must be counted in n) is a carriage control character. Your installation will provide further information on this facility. In this book a blank will always be left immediately after H.

This specification can be used by itself:

    WRITE (8,90)
90   FORMAT (23H JULIA ALISON SANDERSON)

or in conjunction with other format specifications:

    WRITE (8,15) A,D,J,E
15   FORMAT (4H A= F5.2,9H D=F6.2,9H J= 14,9H
                                                                                    E= F6.2)

which could output:

A= 12.34   D= 34.56   J= −789   E= −23.45

You will see that a comma need not be used to separate an H specification from the next specification and that spaces can be included in an H format. There are additional features of format specifications which enable great control to be exercised over printed output. A whole array can be printed by a single statement in a similar manner to which it can be read. There is use of the implied DO statement facility (analogous to that used in reading arrays) for printing. You have now however read about the details of FORTRAN which will enable you to translate a BASIC program quickly.

Below are shown examples 1 and 2 from Exercises 7.1, 8.1 and 8.2 in both FORTRAN and BASIC.

          FORTRAN   BASIC

7.1.1

```
         N = 1                       100  LET N = 1
100      A = FLOAT(N)                110  PRINT N,N*N,N↑3,SQR(N),
         WRITE (8,200) N,N*N,                                   N↑(1/3)
                       N*N*N,        120  LET N = N+1
         SQRT(A),A**(1.0/3.0)        130  IF N < 101 THEN 110
200      FORMAT (I4,4X,I8,4X,        999  END
                 I10,2(4X,F7.2))
         N = N+1
         IF N .LT. 101 GO TO 100
         STOP
         END
```

FORTRAN	BASIC

7.1.2

```
        N = 2                 100  LET N = 1
100     R = 1.0/FLOAT(N)      110  PRINT 1/N
        WRITE (8,200) R       120  LET N = N+1
200     FORMAT (F9.6)         130  IF N < 101 THEN 110
        N = N+1               999  END
        IF N .LT. 101 GO TO 100
        STOP
        END
```

8.1.1

```
        DO 1,N = 1,100           100  FOR N = 1 TO 100
        M = N**2                 110  LET M = N*N
        SQRT A = FLOAT(N)        120  PRINT N,M,M*N,SQR(N),
        WRITE (8,2) N,M,M*N,                              N↑(1/3)
        SQRT(A),A**(1.0/3.0)     130  NEXT N
2       FORMAT (I4,4X,I8,4X,     999  END
                I10,2(4X,F7.2))
1       CONTINUE
        STOP
        END
```

8.1.2

```
        DO 1,N = 2,100           100  FOR N = 2 TO 100
        A = FLOAT(N)             110  PRINT 1/N
        WRITE (8,2)1.0/A         120  NEXT N
2       FORMAT (F9.6)            999  END
1       CONTINUE
        STOP
        END
```

8.2.1

```
        DIMENSION A(10)          100  (Data List)
        TOTAL = 0.               110  LET T = 0
        READ (6,1) A             120  LET N = 1 TO 10
```

From BASIC to FORTRAN

FORTRAN		BASIC
8.2.1, continued		
1 FORMAT (10(F4.2,2X))	130	READ A(N)
DO 2 N = 1,10	140	LET T = T+A(N)
TOTAL = TOTAL + A(N)	150	NEXT N
2 CONTINUE	160	LET V = A/10
AVE = TOTAL/10.0	170	LET D = 0
DEV = 0.	180	FOR J = 1 TO 10
DO 4 J = 1,10	190	IF D > ABS(V−A(J))
Y = ABS(AVE −A(J))		THEN 220
IF DEV .GE. Y GO TO 4	200	LET D = ABS(V−A(J))
DEV = Y	210	LET D1 = A(J)
D = A(J)	220	NEXT J
4 CONTINUE	230	PRINT V,D1
WRITE (8,3)AVE,D	999	END
3 FORMAT (2(F4.2,10X))		
STOP		
END		

8.2.2

DIMENSION X(5,3)	100	DIM X(5,3)
BIG = X(1,1)	120	LET B = X(1,1)
DO 1 I = 1,5	130	FOR I = 1 TO 5
DO 1 J = 1,3	140	FOR J = 1 TO 3
IF X(I,J) .GT. BIG GO TO 2	150	IF X(I,J) > B THEN 170
BIG = X(I,J)	160	LET B = X(I,J)
1 CONTINUE	170	NEXT J
DO 2 I = 1,5	180	NEXT I
DO 2 J = 1,3	190	MAT X = (1.0/B)*X
X(I,J) = X(I,J)/BIG		
2 CONTINUE		

SUGGESTED SOLUTIONS

There are an infinite number of correct solutions to a programming problem. There are innumerable different combinations of the 286 variable identifiers in BASIC which can be used in equally correct solutions, whilst the order of elements of arithmetic expressions and of some program statements can in many cases be altered without prejudice to the final result.

There may also be considerable variation in the number of remarks which are inserted as program statements. The use of these should not be neglected, yet if your program is for your own use only there is not the need for the detail of remarks appropriate to a program for common use.

The suggested solutions have not included checks on the validity of the input since it is assumed that they will be run at a terminal where the user will have carefully checked his input before operating the program. If programs are to be punched and run in the batch-processing mode or they are to be operated by persons other than their author it is advisable to include more stringent checks on the range and type of the input. If data is to be inserted by INPUT statements a message should indicate to the operator the size and form of the desired insertion. These solutions have been tested on a computer. Features such as the multiple assignment statement and the ON GO TO statement which are not common to all versions of BASIC are not included in the solutions. In all cases the use of ingenious short cuts, which may well occur to you, have been avoided.

Suggested Solutions

Exercises 5.1

1.
```
100  LET A = 1017
110  LET B = 43
120  PRINT A,B,A+B+B,A+A,B−A
999  END
```

2.
```
10   LET X0 = 19
20   LET Y  = 7
40   LET A1 = −6
50   LET B  = 8
60   PRINT X0,Y,Y+B
70   PRINT
90   PRINT A1 +X0
999  END
```

3.
```
100  LET A = 17
110  LET B = 5
120  PRINT A+A+B+B+B
999  END
```

4.
```
100  LET A = 17
110  LET B = 5
120  PRINT A
130  PRINT
140  PRINT B
150  PRINT
160  PRINT A+A+B+B+B
999  END
```

5.
```
100  LET A = 18
110  LET Z = 8
120  LET X = A
130  LET A = Z
140  LET Z = X
```

```
150   PRINT Z,A
160   PRINT A,Z
999   END
```

Exercises 6.1

1.
```
 90   REM LINES 110,120,140,170,180,190,200,210,220
                                              CHANGED
100   LET A = 7
110   LET B = 5
120   LET C = 1000
130   LET E = (A↑3)
140   LET D = 2.0
150   LET E = −E
160   LET D = D + 1
170   LET F = 4*(C+D)
180   LET G = A*(B+E↑(5−D))
190   LET H = G*(−E)
200   PRINT
210   LET K = H↑(+2)
220   PRINT E,F,G,H
99999 END
```

2.

$$K = 2, \ D = 139, \ E = 3, F = 633$$

3.
```
100   LET A = 43
110   LET B = 52
120   LET C = 3260
130   LET X = 2
140   PRINT A*X↑2 +B*X +C
999   END
```

4.
```
100   PRINT 1,2,3,4
110   PRINT 1,1/2,1/3,1/4
120   PRINT 1*1,2*2,3*3,4*4
```

```
         130   PRINT 1↑3,2↑3,3↑3,4↑3
         999   END
```

5.
```
         100   LET P = 2
         110   LET Q = 3
         120   LET R = 4
         130   LET A = P↑2
         140   LET B = Q↑2
         150   LET C = P*Q
         160   LET D = Q*R
         170   LET X = ((C+D)/(A+B))/((B−D)/(A+C))
         180   PRINT X
         999   END
```

6.
```
         100   LET Y = (81−4*5*(−6))↑.5
         110   PRINT (9+Y)/(2*5), (9−Y)/(2*5)
         999   END
```

7.
```
         100   PRINT (65↑2 + 72↑2)↑.5
         999   END
```

8.
```
         100   PRINT 6.28* (200/980.67)↑.5
         999   END
```

Exercises 6.2

1.
```
         100   REM MESSAGE FOR OPERATOR
         110   PRINT "TYPE A POSITIVE INTEGER."
         120   INPUT N
         130   PRINT
         140   PRINT
         150   PRINT "NUMBER","SQUARE","CUBE","RECIP.",
                                                 "ROOT"
         160   PRINT N,N*N,N*N*N,1/N,SQR(N)
         999   END
```

Suggested Solutions

2.

All the following programs should be preceded by an appropriate DATA list in line 100 and concluded by an END statement in line 999.

a.
```
110   READ P,R
120   LET A = 2*P*R* SIN(3.14/P)
130   PRINT A
```

b.
```
110   READ B,C
120   LET A = 2*SQR(B*B +(4*C↑2/3))
130   PRINT A
```

c.
```
110   READ P,Y
120   LET A = −COS(Y)↑ (P+1)/(P+1)
130   PRINT A
```

d.
```
110   READ X
120   REM SINE.COMPUTED ONLY ONCE
130   LET Y = SIN(X)
140   LET A = .5*LOG((1+Y)/(1−Y))
150   PRINT A
```

e.
```
110   READ X
120   LET A = (2/(3.14*X))↑.5* SIN(X)
130   PRINT A
```

f.
```
110   READ B,E,H,P
120   LET A = E*H*P/(SIN(B)*(H↑4/16 +(H*P)↑2)
130   PRINT A
```

g.
```
110   READ B,S,X
120   LET A = X*S/2 −B↑ 2/2*LOG(ABS(X+S))
130   PRINT A
```

Suggested Solutions

h.
```
110   READ X,B,C,D,E,F,H,I,J,K,M,N,P,Q
120   LET A = (X−B/C/(D−E↑(F+Q)))/(H↑I↑(J−K)+Q↑
                                         (M/(N+P)))
130   PRINT A
```

i.
```
110   READ E,F,L,C,R
120   LET A = E/ (SQR(R↑2+ (6.28*F*L−.5*3.14*F*C)))
```

3.
```
100   REM MESSAGE FOR OPERATOR
110   PRINT "TYPE THE 3 ANGLES"
120   INPUT A,B,C
130   LET F = 3.141593/180
140   LET A = A*F
150   LET B = B*F
160   LET C = C*F
170   LET E =(A+B+C−3.141593)/2
180   LET S = SIN(E)
190   LET S1 = SIN(A−E)
200   LET S2= SIN(B−E)
210   LET S3= SIN(C−E)
220   LET P = SQR(S/(S1*S2*S3))
230   LET A1= 2*ATN(S1*P)/F
240   LET A2= 2*ATN(S2*P)/F
250   LET A3= 2*ATN(S3*P)/F
260   PRINT A1,A2,A3
999   END
```

Exercises 7.1

1.
```
100   LET N = 1
110   PRINT N,N*N,N*N*N,SQR(N),N↑(1/3)
120   LET N = N+1
130   IF N< 101 THEN 110
999   END
```

2.
```
100  LET N = 2
110  PRINT 1/N
120  LET N = N+1
130  IF N <101 THEN 110
999  END
```

3.
```
100  (Data list)
110  LET T = 0
120  LET K = 0
130  REM T = TOTAL,K = COUNT
140  READ N
150  LET T = N+T
160  LET K = K+1
170  IF K <10 THEN 140
180  PRINT "MEAN =",T/10
999  END
```

4.
```
100  (Data list)
110  LET C = 0
120  REM C = COUNT
130  READ A,B
140  PRINT (SQR(A↑2+B↑2))
150  LET C = C+1
160  IF C < 10 THEN 130
999  END
```

5.
```
100  LET A = 1
110  PRINT A, SQR(A/3.14)
120  LET A = A+1
130  IF A < 101 THEN 110
999  END
```

6.
```
100  LET P = 0
110  LET K1= 0
120  LET K2= 0
```

```
130  LET N = 1
140  LET T = 1
150  LET T = SGN(T)*1/N
160  LET P = P+T
170  LET N = N+2
180  LET T = -T
190  LET K2= K2+1
200  IF K2<100 THEN 150
210  LET K2= 0
220  PRINT 4*P
230  LET K1= K1 +1
240  IF K1 < 10 THEN 150
999  END
```

7.
```
100  LET N1 = 0
110  LET N2 = 1
120  LET N3 = N2 +N1
130  LET N1 = N2
140  LET N2 = N3
150  IF N3 < 10↑3 THEN 120
160  IF N3 > 10↑6 THEN 999
170  PRINT N3
180  GO TO 120
999  END
```

8.
```
100  REM MESSAGE FOR OPERATOR
110  PRINT "TYPE 6 NUMBERS"
120  INPUT A,B,C,P,Q,R
130  PRINT
140  LET D = A*Q-B*P
150  LET E = B*R-C*Q
160  IF D = 0 THEN 210
170  LET X = E/D
180  LET Y = (P*C-A*R)/D
190  PRINT X,Y
200  STOP
210  IF E <> 0 THEN 240
220  PRINT "NOT INDEPENDENT "
```

```
230  STOP
240  PRINT "INDETERMINATE"
999  END
```

Exercises 8.1

1.
```
100  FOR N = 1 TO 100
110  PRINT N,N*N,N*N*N,SQR(N),N↑(1/3)
120  NEXT N
999  END
```

2.
```
100  FOR N = 2 TO 100
110  PRINT 1/N
120  NEXT N
999  END
```

3.
```
100  (Data list)
110  REM T = TOTAL
120  LET T = 0
130  FOR K = 1 TO 10
140  READ X
150  LET T = T+X
160  NEXT K
170  PRINT T/10
999  END
```

4.
```
100  (Data list)
110  FOR K = 1 TO 10
120  READ X,Y
130  PRINT SQR(X↑2+Y↑2)
140  NEXT K
999  END
```

Suggested Solutions

5.
```
100  FOR A = 1 TO 100
110  PRINT A,SQR(A/3.14)
120  NEXT A
999  END
```

6.
```
100  LET N = 1
110  LET T = 1
120  LET P = 0
130  FOR K = 1 TO 10
140  FOR L = 1 TO 100
150  LET P = SGN(T)*1/N+P
160  LET T = -T
170  LET N = N+2
180  NEXT L
190  PRINT "AFTER",K*100,"TERMS","PI IS ",4*P
200  NEXT K
999  END
```

Exercises 8.2

1.
```
100  (Data list)
110  LET T = 0
120  FOR N = 1 TO 10
130  READ A(N)
140  LET T = T+A(N)
150  NEXT N
160  LET M = T/10
170  LET D = 0
180  FOR J = 1 TO 10
190  IF D > ABS(A(J)-M) THEN 220
200  LET D = ABS(A(J)-M)
210  LET D1 = A(J)
220  NEXT J
230  PRINT M,D1
999  END
```

2.

```
100   DIM X(5,3)
120   LET B = X(1,1)
130   FOR I = 1 TO 5
140   FOR J = 1 TO 3
150   IF X(I,J) > B THEN 170
160   LET B = X(I,J)
170   NEXT J
180   NEXT I
190   FOR I = 1 TO 5
200   FOR J = 1 TO 3
210   LET X(I,J) = X(I,J)/B
220   NEXT J
230   NEXT I
999   END
```

3.

```
100   DIM A(3,4)
110   LET B = A(1,1)
120   LET I = 1
130   LET J = 1
140   FOR K = 1 TO 3
150   FOR L = 1 TO 4
160   IF A(K,L) > B THEN 210
170   NEXT L
180   NEXT K
190   PRINT B,I,J
200   STOP
210   LET I = K
220   LET J = L
230   LET B = A(K,L)
240   GO TO 170
999   END
```

4.

```
100   DIM P(50)
110   LET I = 1
120   LET J = 3
130   LET P(1) = 3
140   LET K = 0
```

Suggested Solutions

```
150    LET K = K+1
160    IF P(K) <= INT(SQR(J)) THEN 230
170    PRINT J
180    LET P(I) = J
190    LET I = I+1
200    LET J = J+2
210    IF J < 100 THEN 140
220    STOP
230    LET M = INT(J/P(K))
240    IF J = P(K)*M THEN 200
250    GO TO 150
999    END
```

5.
```
100    DIM A(10)
110    FOR M = 1 TO 5
120    LET A(M) = M
130    LET A(M+5) = M
140    NEXT M
150    FOR N = 0 TO 4
160    PRINT A(N+1),A(N+2),A(N+3),A(N+4),A(N+5)
170    NEXT N
999    END
```

6.
```
100    (Data list)
120    LET L = 0
130    LET M = 1000
140    LET T = 0
150    REM L = LARGEST,M = SMALLEST,T = TOTAL
160    LET K = 1
170    REM K = COUNT
180    READ X
190    IF X = -1 THEN 270
200    LET T = T+X
210    LET K = K+1
220    IF L > X THEN 240
230    LET L = X
240    IF M < X THEN 260
250    LET M = X
```

```
260  GO TO 180
270  PRINT "MEAN","LARGEST","SMALLEST"
280  PRINT T/K,L,M
999  END
```

7.
```
100  (Data list)
110  LET K = 0
120  REM K = COUNT
130  READ X
140  IF X = 0 THEN 180
150  IF SGN(X) <> -1 THEN 130
160  LET K = K+1
170  GO TO 130
180  PRINT K, "NEGATIVE NUMBERS"
999  END
```

8.
```
100  (Data list)
110  DIM A(5,3)
120  PRINT "ORIGINAL MATRIX."
130  FOR M = 1 TO 5
140  FOR N = 1 TO 3
150  READ A(M,N)
160  NEXT N
170  PRINT A(M,1),A(M,2),A(M,3)
180  NEXT M
190  FOR L = 1 TO 3
200  LET X = A(1,L)
210  LET A(1,L) = A(3,L)
220  LET A(3,L) = X
230  NEXT L
240  PRINT "ALTERED MATRIX."
250  FOR M = 1 TO 5
260  PRINT A(M,1),A(M,2),A(M,3)
270  NEXT M
999  END
```

Suggested Solutions 151

Exercises 9.1

1.
All the exercises a–f have the following common statements:

```
110   (Data list of 3 items)
120   DIM E(4)
130   REM MESSAGE FOR OPERATOR
140   PRINT "INPUT A POSITIVE NUMBER"
150   INPUT E(4)
160   FOR I = 1 TO 3
170   READ E(I)
180   NEXT I
190   FOR K = 1 TO 4
200   PRINT FNA(E(K))
210   NEXT K
999   END
```

a.
```
100   DEF FNA(X) = LOG(X)/LOG(10)
```
b.
```
100   DEF FNA(X) = TAN(X*.0174533)
```
c.
```
100   DEF FNA(X) = 3.141593*X↑2
```
d.
```
100   DEF FNA(X) = X*.0174533
```
e.
```
100   DEF FNA(X) = INT(X+ .5)
```
f.
```
100   DEF FNA(X) = X↑.333333
```

2.
```
100   REM CLEAR COUNTERS 1-6
110   DIM N(6)
120   FOR K = 1 TO 6
130   LET N(K) = 0
140   NEXT K
150   FOR M = 1 TO 100
160   LET X = INT(6*RND(1))+1
170   LET N(X) = N(X) + 1
```

```
180   NEXT M
190   REM PRINTS COUNTS 1-6
200   FOR K = 1 TO 6
210   PRINT N(K)
220   NEXT K
999   END
```

3.
```
100   REM RANDOM NO. INDICATES VALUE OF CARD. SUITS ARE
110   REM HTS. 1-13,DIA.14-26,CLUBS, 27-39,SP. 40-52 SO THAT
120   REM 7 CLUBS WOULD HAVE VALUE OF 33
130   FOR K = 1 TO 13
140   LET X = INT(52* RND(1)) +1
150   REM CALCULATE SUIT INDICATOR
160   LET A = INT(X/13.3)
170   LET B = X-13*A
180   REM B IS POSITION IN SUIT
190   IF B = 1 THEN 300
200   IF B =12 THEN 320
210   IF B =13 THEN 340
220   IF B =11 THEN 360
230   PRINT B, "OF"
240   IF A = 0 THEN 380
250   IF A = 1 THEN 400
260   IF A = 2 THEN 420
270   PRINT "SPADES"
280   NEXT K
290   STOP
300   PRINT "ACE OF"
310   GO TO 240
320   PRINT "QUEEN OF"
330   GO TO 240
340   PRINT "KING OF"
350   GO TO 240
360   PRINT "JACK OF"
370   GO TO 240
380   PRINT "HEARTS"
390   GO TO 280
```

```
400  PRINT "DIAMONDS"
410  GO TO 280
420  PRINT "CLUBS"
430  GO TO 280
440  REM ON GO TO NOT USED AS NOT IN ALL
                           VERSIONS OF BASIC
999  END
```

4.
```
100  PRINT "PAIR","IMPAIR","MANQUE","PASSE"
110  REM CLEAR COUNTERS
120  LET A = 0
130  LET B = 0
140  LET C = 0
150  LET D = 0
160  REM MULTIPLE ASSIGNT. COULD BE USED ABOVE—
                        NOT COMMON TO ALL BASIC
170  FOR K = 1 TO 1000
180  LET X = INT(36*RND(1)) +1
190  IF X < 19 THEN 260
200  LET D = D+1
210  IF X−2*INT(X/2) = 0 THEN 280
220  LET B = B+1
230  NEXT K
240  PRINT A,B,C,D
250  STOP
260  LET C = C+1
270  GO TO 210
280  LET A = A+1
290  GO TO 230
999  END
```

5.
```
100  (Data list)
110  DIM A(10)
120  FOR K = 1 TO 10
130  READ A(K)
140  NEXT K
150  REM ARRAY SIZE TO BE IN Z9
160  LET Z9 = 10
```

```
170   GOSUB 6000
180   GOSUB 7000
190   PRINT "MAXIMUM = ",Z8,"MINIMUM =",Z7
200   STOP
210   REM MAXIMUM SUBROUTINE
6000  LET Z8 = A(1)
6010  FOR Y = 2 TO Z9
6020  IF Z8 > A(Y) THEN 6040
6030  LET Z8 = A(Y)
6040  NEXT Y
6050  RETURN
6999  REM MINIMUM SUBROUTINE
7000  LET Z7 = A(1)
7010  FOR Y = 2 TO Z9
7020  IF Z8 < A(Y) THEN 7040
7030  LET Z7 = A(Y)
7040  NEXT Y
7050  RETURN
9999  END
```

6.
```
100   (Data list)
110   REM DATA LIST ITEMS TO BE POSITIVE
120   FOR K = 1 TO 10
130   READ A(K)
140   GOSUB 900
150   PRINT A(K),"RADIANS = ", Z9,Z8,Z7
160   NEXT K
170   STOP
180   REM SUBROUTINE STARTS BELOW
900   LET Z9 = A(K)* 57.2958
910   IF Z9 <= 360 THEN 940
920   LET Z9 = Z9 -360
930   GO TO 910
940   LET Z6 = INT(Z9)
950   LET Z6 = (Z9 - Z6)*60
960   LET Z8 = INT(Z6)
970   LET Z7 = INT((Z6-Z8)*60 + .5)
980   RETURN
999   END
```

Suggested Solutions 155

7.
```
100   (Data list)
110   READ A,B,C
120   GOSUB 700
130   STOP
140   REM START OF SUBROUTINE
700   LET Z8 = B*B − 4*A*C
710   IF Z8 <>0 THEN 740
720   PRINT "ONLY ONE SOLUTION, X = ",−B/(2*A)
730   RETURN
740   IF Z8 < 0 THEN 770
750   PRINT "X =",(−B +SQR(Z8))/(2*A), "AND",
                               (−B−SQR(Z8))/(2*A))
760   RETURN
770   PRINT "IMAGINARY SOLUTIONS"
780   RETURN
999   END
```

8.
```
100   REM USED ON TEN NUMBERS
110   (Data list)
120   FOR K = 1 TO 10
130   READ Z8
140   GOSUB 700
150   NEXT K
160   STOP
170   REM START OF SUBROUTINE
700   PRINT "FACTORS OF",Z8,"LISTED ON LINES
                                       BELOW."
710   DATA 2,3,5,7
720   FOR Z = 1 TO 4
730   READ Y(Z)
740   NEXT Z
750   RESTORE
760   EOR Z = 1 TO 4
770   LET Z7 = Z8/Y(Z)
780   IF Z8 <> Z7*Y(Z) THEN 830
790   PRINT Y(Z)
800   IF Z7 = 1 THEN 850
810   LET Z8 = Z7
```

```
820  GO TO 770
830  NEXT Z
840  PRINT Z8
850  RETURN
999  END
```

Exercises 10.1

1.
```
100  (Data list)
110  DIM A$(5),B$(5)
120  LET D$ = "ZZZZZZ"
130  FOR N = 1 TO 5
140  READ A$(N)
150  NEXT N
160  FOR M = 1 TO 5
170  LET E$ = D$
180  LET L = 1
190  FOR N= 1 TO 5
195  IF A$(N) >= E$ THEN 220
200  LET E$ = A$(N)
210  LET L = N
220  NEXT N
230  LET A$(L) = D$
240  LET B$(M) = E$
250  NEXT M
260  FOR K = 1 TO 5
270  PRINT B$(K)
280  NEXT K
999  END
```

2.
```
100  (Data list)
110  DIM H$ (30)
120  LET K = 1
130  READ H$(K)
140  IF H$ (K) = "." THEN 170
150  LET K= K+1
160  GO TO 130
170  PRINT K-1, "WORDS"
999  END
```

Suggested Solutions

3.
```
100  DIM A$(13)
110  DATA "ACE","2","3","4","5","6","7","8","9","10",
                                              "JACK"
120  DATA "QUEEN","KING","HEARTS","DIAMONDS",
                                  "CLUBS","SPADES"
130  FOR K = 1 TO 17
140  READ A$(K)
150  NEXT K
160  REM CARD DESCRPNS. & SUITS READ TO ARRAY
170  REM RANDOM NOS. USED AS IN EXERCISE 9.1.3.
180  REM HAND NOW DEALT
190  FOR N = 1 TO 10
200  LET X = INT(52*RND(1)) +1
210  REM CALCULATE SUIT NOW
220  LET Y = INT(X/13.3)
230  LET Z =Y + 14
240  REM NOW POSITION IN SUIT CALCULATED
250  LET W = X – 13*Y
260  PRINT X;A$(W);"OF";A$(Z)
270  NEXT N
999  END
```

4.
```
100  REM N USED FOR ASSEMBLY OF NUMBER
110  LET N = 0
120  REM READ DECODE TABLE
130  DATA "0","1","2","3","4","5","6","7","8","9"
140  DIM E$(10)
150  FOR K = 1 TO 10
160  READ E$(K)
170  NEXT K
180  REM START OF MAIN PROGRAM
190  PRINT "INPUT SINGLE INTEGER OR * TO END
                                          DIGITS."
200  INPUT X$
210  IF X$= "*" THEN 280
220  REM DECODE LOOP
230  FOR K = 1 TO 10
240  IF X$ = E$(K) THEN 260
```

```
250   NEXT K
260   LET N = 10*N+K−1
270   GO TO 190
280   PRINT
290   PRINT "NUMBER = "; N;"SQ. =";N*N;"ROOT = ";
                                                  SQR(N)
999   END
```

5.
```
100   (Data list)
110   FOR K = 1 TO 10
120   READ N
130   PRINT N;
140   FOR M = 1 TO N
150   PRINT "+";
160   NEXT M
170   PRINT
180   NEXT K
999   END
```

6.
```
100   (Data item)
110   READ N
120   DATA "ZERO","ONE","TWO","THREE","FOUR",
130   DATA "FIVE", "SIX", "SEVEN", "EIGHT", "NINE"
140   FOR K = 1 TO 10
150   READ X$(K)
160   NEXT K
170   LET R = N − 11*INT (N/11)
180   PRINT X$(N+1)
999   END
```

INDEX

ABS, 62
Absolute value, 62
Addition, 47, 55
ALGOL 60, 28–30, 33, 43
Algorithm, 33
Arctangent, 62
Arithmetic expression, 55–64
Arithmetic unit, 6, 13
Arrays,
    dimensions, 90–92
    name, 91
    string, 110
Assembly languages, 26–27
Assignment statement, *see* LET
ATN, 62
Auxiliary memory, *see* Backing store

Babbage, Charles, 5
Backing store, 11–13
Batch-processing, 8, 44
Binary, 25
Brackets, *see* Parentheses
Burroughs, 122
Byte, 10–11

CALL (FORTRAN), 129–131
CATALOG, 46
CDC, 122
Central processor, 7
Character manipulation, 108–113
Checkout, *see* Program testing
COBOL, 28–29
Comparisons, 72–73
Compilers, 13
Computer Technology Ltd., 122
Conditional statements, 73–80, 112–113
Constants
    numeric, 51–52
    string, 67, 109
CONTINUE (FORTRAN), 128

Control unit, 6, 14–15
Core store, 10
COS, 62
Cosine, 62
Counts, 76
CPU, *see* Central processor
Cycle time, 11

Data, 64–66, 110
Data transmission, 21–24
Datel facilities, 21–22
DEF, 95–97
Disc storage, 12
DIM, 90–92, 110, 115
DIMENSION (FORTRAN), 129
Division, 56
DO (FORTRAN), 128–129

Encoders, 9
END, 48
END (FORTRAN), 131
Error correction, 46
EXP, 62
Exponentiation symbol, 56

File store, *see* Backing store
Floating point, 13–14
Flowcharts, 34–38
FORMAT (FORTRAN), 132–135
FOR-TO, 84–89
FORTRAN, 28–29, 32, 43, 123–137
Functions
    (FORTRAN), 131–132
    self-defined, *see* DEF
    standard, 61–64, 97, 100

GOSUB, 101
GO TO, 70–72
GO TO ON, *see* ON GO TO

High-level languages, 27–31
Honeywell, 122

IBM Call 360, 122
IBM System 3, 122
ICL 1900 series, 122
IF (FORTRAN), 127–128
IF-THEN, 73–80, 112–113
INPUT, 66, 68, 111
Input media, 8–9
INT, 62–64
Iterative techniques, 78–80

Jump, see GO TO

Kemeny, J. G., 43
Kurtz, T. E., 43

LET, 49–50, 55–64
Line
    deletion, 46
    format, 48–49
    length, 48
    number, 47–48
Line-printer, 10
LIST, 48
LOG, 62
Logarithm, 62–63
Loops, 33–34, 76–80, 84–89
Loops (FORTRAN), 128–129
Low-level languages, see Assembly languages

Machine language, 25–26
Magnetic discs, see Disc storage
Magnetic drums, 13
Magnetic tape, 9, 12
Main store, see Store
MAT statements, 115–120
Matrix instructions, see MAT statements
Memory, see Store
Multiple assignment statements, 59–60, 125
Multiplexor, 23
Multiplication, 56
Multi-programming, 16–17

NEW, 44–45
NEXT, see FOR-TO

OLD, 44–45
Operating systems, 16–19
Output, 6, 9–10

Paper tape, 8

Parentheses, 57–59
PDP, 122
PRINT, 52–54, 67–68, 106–108
    with commas, 52–54, 67–68
    with semi-colons, 106–108
Printer, see Line-printer
Program, 4
Program testing, 37–**41**
Pseudo-random numbers, 97
Punched card, 9

Random numbers, 97–100
READ, 64–66
READ (FORTRAN), 132–134
READY, 45
Relational operators, 72–73
REM, 49
RENAME, 46
RESTORE, 66
RETURN, 101
RETURN (FORTRAN), 130
RND, 97–100
Rounding, 63–64
RUN, 46–47

SAVE, 46
SGN, 62
SIN, 62
Sine, 62
Space
    in statements, 48
    in strings, 109
Square root, 62
SQR, 62
STOP, 75
STOP (FORTRAN), 131
Store, 6, 10–11
String
    constant, 67, 109
    variable, 110
Subroutines, 30, 100–104
Subroutines (FORTRAN), 129–131
Subscripted variables, see Arrays
Subtraction, 47, 55
System commands, 44–46

TAB, 108
TAN, 62
Tangent, 62
Teletype, 9, 19–20, 44–45
Terminal, 16–21, 44–45
Typewriter, see Teletype

Index

UNIVAC, 5, 122
UNSAVE, 46

Variable
  (FORTRAN), 125−126
  numeric, 50−51

Variable (contd)
  string, 110
VDU, 10, 20−21
Visual display unit, *see* VDU

WRITE (FORTRAN), 134−135

RENEW CALL 462-6950
DATE DUE